I0796786

TO

FROM

DATE

HEAVEN MEETS EARTH

A 40-DAY JOURNEY OF TRANSFORMATION THROUGH THE NICENE CREED

JOSH NADEAU

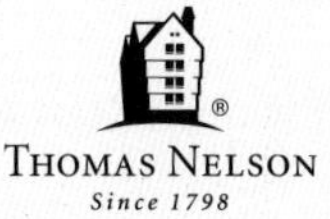

THOMAS NELSON
Since 1798

TO RANSOM,

WHOSE NAME IS A PROMISE,

WHOSE PATH LAYS BEFORE HIM.

CONTENTS

THE NICENE CREED

I believe in one God, Father Almighty,
Creator of heaven and earth,
and of all things visible and invisible.

And in one Lord Jesus Christ,
the only-begotten Son of God,
begotten of the Father before all ages;
Light of Light, true God of true God,
begotten, not created, of one essence with the Father
through Whom all things were made.
Who for us men and for our salvation
came down from heaven
and was incarnate of the Holy Spirit
and the Virgin Mary and became man.
He was crucified for us under Pontius Pilate,
and suffered and was buried;
And He rose on the third day,
according to the Scriptures.

He ascended into heaven
and is seated at the right hand of the Father;
And He will come again with glory
to judge the living and dead.
His kingdom shall have no end.

And in the Holy Spirit,
the Lord, the Creator of life,
Who proceeds from the Father,
Who together with the Father
and the Son
is worshipped and glorified,
Who spoke through the prophets.

In one, holy, catholic, and apostolic Church.

I confess one baptism for the forgiveness of sins.

I look for the resurrection of the dead,
and the life of the age to come.

Amen.

LET THERE BE . . .

If you stop for a moment, you can hear it.

If you turn down the noise, if you slow the rush, if you shut off the screens.

If you take a breath, if you close your eyes.

And if you stay in that moment, that tense silence of solitude, if you linger in stillness, just a little while, it will beckon you:

the whisper of eternity.

Late have I loved you, Beauty so ancient and so new,
late have I loved you! Lo, you were within, but I outside,

> seeking there for you, and upon the shapely things you have made I rushed headlong—I, misshapen. You were with me, but I was not with you.
>
> St. Augustine[1]

I remember when I heard it most clearly.

It was early morning, and the TV screen in the station showed that our train was on time to leave for Austria. People all around were shuffling off and buying tickets and getting baggage settled, and we, my wife and I, were eating some apples we had bought at the market the day before. There was the murmur of voices, the clack and hiss of engines settling to a stop, and then a voice over the intercom. It was announcing something, but I don't speak German, so I double-checked the screen to make sure we were on the right platform. We had spent a few days in Munich, and now we were off to visit friends in the far west of Austria near the border of Switzerland.

Our train arrived, and soon we were rolling through the winding tracks of Southern Bavaria into the sharp mountainous landscape. The car rocked and swayed, and out the window were trees and the rugged lines of blue peaks and cleft stone.

It was a small town, our destination, and when we arrived, my friend and his cousin were waiting for my wife and me on the platform. They grabbed our bags, tossed them in the trunk of the car, and filled us in on the plans for the evening.

"We're going to climb a mountain for sunset," said my friend's cousin. "We can have a bonfire up there on the summit."

They told us that normally we would need a permit to climb this mountain because it had been gated off. But since the cousin worked in the mayor's office, we got special permission. When the time came, we drove to the gated road, unlocked the chain, and headed to a small lot. There were six of us, three couples, and we laced up our boots, grabbed our packs, and began the climb.

It was rolling greens of long grass, swaying on the wind, and an amber dirt path that cut through, curving round and round and up and up. Dusk was slowly settling in, and the sky was transforming from clear and bright blues to the soft golds of early evening. The grit of the earth crunched under our boots, and it was this drumming rhythm, our twelve feet marching along. We slowly crested a hill, and there were these giant steel beams, rust red, welded together in giant Xs, some twenty feet tall, in rows of five or so, dotted all over the mountainside. Sweat beaded on my brow.

"What are these?" I asked.

"Those are to break up the avalanches," the cousin said. "The snow will get stuck in them and split apart, and that will stop it from crashing down upon the village."

Flowers grew at their bases, and also along the steep mountainside ridges. The air was fresh and wild, almost like we were the first humans to leave our scent up there. I knew this wasn't true; someone had to carve the path and place those giant steel trusses. But when I breathed in, I felt like I could smell life from some three hundred years ago.

History lingered there, and you could fill your lungs with it.

It wasn't a marked history—there were no tomes written about the travelers of this mountain. No, this was like a mythology, an untamed lore, something you could only feel. And our little fellowship followed those same travelers' steps, surrounded by sprawling Alpine peaks, jagged and navy, cobalt stone reaching up into the golden sky.

The climb took a while, but we reached the summit and offloaded our packs. The guys carried the firewood and the drinks, and the girls carried the food. We built our fire, opened our bottles of beer, and cooked our sausages on the cast-iron skillet placed over the flickering flames. And then we waited, watching the sun slowly descend to a set.

In celebratory silence.

It was too much, almost, to take in.

Around us, as far as the eye could see, were mountains, the last beams of day casting shadows on their silent fissures. I assumed they were all just as wild and just as beautiful as this one. Just as untouched, just as alive. We looked for other bonfires, beacons, some proof that others were enjoying the same majesty we were.

But there were none.

Maybe that night we stood alone under the ferocious nobility of the Alpine twilight. And it made sense to me, then, why ancients believed that these places, these mountain summits, were where heaven and earth overlapped.

Because it was true.

I was, by all rights, standing in the heavens.

And if I squinted hard enough, I felt like I could see the divine. Like in that moment, the King of the mountain was immanent, just beyond my reach. But I could sense Him, His fullness, His beauty, and it was overwhelming.

It was a moment that felt eternal.

CONCEPTS CREATE IDOLS: ONLY WONDER COMPREHENDS ANYTHING . . . WONDER MAKES US FALL TO OUR KNEES.

GREGORY OF NYSSA[2]

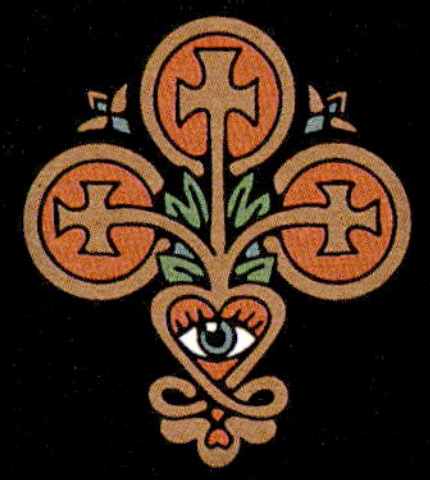

WAYS OF SEEING

Somehow, we've grown suspicious of the eternal.

In our modern time, we have sought to tear down these ancient peaks, the places where heaven and earth overlap, and in their rubble we have built little strip malls. We have tried our best to replace every last bit of mythos in our world with cold, hard facts. We have replaced the King of the mountain and His wild beauty with scientific laws and chemical compositions, with spreadsheets and factories, with productivity apps, and calendar notifications, and curated feeds. We have built new mountains—digital ones, intellectual ones, emotional ones—chasing transcendence on our own terms.

Not His terms.

His ways are untamed, and that won't do for sophisticated twenty-first-century folk like us. No, we would like to schedule when heaven can meet earth, and we would like to make God in our image.

"The only palliative is to keep the clean sea breeze of the centuries blowing through our minds, and this can be done only by reading old books," C. S. Lewis wrote in his introduction to Athanasius's *On the Incarnation.*[1] And he was right—both of them were: Lewis in the twentieth century, Athanasius, Bishop of Alexandria, in the fourth. I believe there is a way to breathe the ancient air of heaven again. A way to fill our lungs with wild beauty—and be transformed by beholding.

I believe there is a way to see clearly again.

The Nicene Creed.

This Creed is ancient air—breathed out by the early church, a signal fire from the summit. In it, and by it, you can smell that eternal kind of life—the same life that has lingered in the lungs of the saints since our Christ conquered death. The Creed is more than doctrine; it is direction—an amber trail carved through centuries of questions and doubts and fractures. It is a place where heaven and earth still meet.

To know the Creed, to be formed by it, is to return to those high places. To return to the sacred space where our vision is clear, the air is thin, and the Holy Spirit draws near. It is to breathe the clean sea breeze of the centuries, to fill our lungs with wild beauty and be transformed.

The Creed is old—some 1,700 years old—first written in AD 325 at the Council of Nicaea, then affirmed and expanded in AD 381 at Constantinople. These councils gathered to wrestle with, and clarify, the deepest questions around the nature of Christ, confronting the heresy of Arianism:

Was He truly God?

Truly man?

And how was it that the infinite could incarnate into the finite and yet remain *both*?

The Creed is not abstract. It is not simply left to the world of ideas or the life of the mind. It had expression. It was a shield against heresy—like Arianism, a teaching that claimed Jesus was a created being and not fully God. Each line of the Creed was deliberate and fought for. It was a boundary against theological distortion and a refuge against all the winds of confusion. And the Creed was lived; it was an embodied part of life. It was spoken before baptisms, chanted in monasteries and cathedrals, sung and cheered.

It was a guide to a soul.

And I hope through these coming pages it will be a guide to you as well.

To lead you up the mountain.

"To find the place where all the beauty came from."[2]

The Creed shows us the way up the mountain, but it will not move our feet. We need to do that ourselves. We need to walk its ancient slopes, up into that glowing firelight of truth, into the transformation of embodied obedience, and there, we encounter life. We need to let the Creed remake and reshape us, to let it fill our lungs with the clean breeze of the ages. And that demands something slow and quiet and habitual.

It requires a practice.

And it is through this framework—one of intimacy and union—that we come to the Nicene Creed. In its phrases are rich theology and philosophy, structured around the Trinity: the Father, the Son, and the Holy Spirit. These truths matter, they always have, and they always will, but our goal isn't just the theology or the philosophy. Our path is different. Not the mere accumulation of doctrines or definitions or defenses. We want *intimacy.* We want to participate in the truth, goodness, and beauty of God.

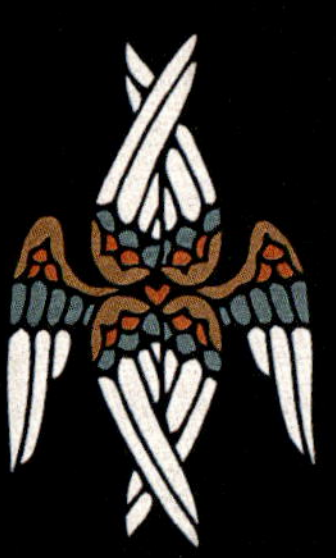

BY WORD AND IMAGE

Vladimir Lossky, the Eastern Orthodox theologian, wrote: "Christian theology is always in the last resort a means: a unity of knowledge subserving an end which transcends all knowledge. This ultimate end is union with God."[1]

And if union with God is our end, then our method must be slow and quiet and habitual. *Method* may not even be the right word. It sounds too analytical, too experimental. Call this a *practice*: a way of framing both body and soul toward the living God.

And to do that we will turn to two ancient rhythms of the church: the *Lectio Divina* and the *Visio Divina*.

LECTIO DIVINA

There is this ancient way of reading the Scriptures: slow, attentive, contemplative. Personal and intimate. A proper means, as it were, toward the ultimate end.

Origen, in the third century AD, called this *contemplative* reading a devotion to the Divine Reading. And over time, this practice, the *Lectio Divina*, was formalized and clarified. It was used as a way for those who follow Jesus to be transformed by enjoying His truth, goodness, and beauty. Formation by intimacy, growth through presence. And its aim is conformity: to become like Christ, to listen to His Spirit as He guides us into all truth, and, then, to be remade.

Let me walk you through the four movements of *Lectio Divina*, and as we start, be silent before the Lord. Take a few quiet minutes to pray. Ask the Holy Spirit to fill you, to prepare you. Then begin.

Lectio

The first movement is the *lectio*, or reading.

Take a short section of Scripture and read it. Slowly. Deliberately. The Benedictine monks, according to their rule of life, read a passage for hours at a time, depending on the liturgical season.

Let the words settle softly into your mind. Read them over, a few times. Let them move from the page to the heart. You are not reading for information; you are listening for familiarity.

Meditatio

The second movement is the *meditatio*, or meditation.

Ponder. Listen. Reflect. Use your senses.

Imagine yourself in the gospel scene. Hear the words; smell the dust; feel the tension, the mercy, the grace. Experience a nearness to Jesus.

Let the Holy Spirit direct you into a place of waiting and receiving. This is not a test; there are no grades; there is no need to rush or scramble for answers or interpretations.

Wait, listen, and expect to hear.

Oratio

The third movement is the *oratio*, or prayer.

Prayer is a conversation with God, and this moment is a response—the invitation of intimacy. Speak to God about all He stirred in you during the time of reading and meditation. Use the words He has given you. This is a response of nearness, and it requires honesty, the kind that comes from clear listening.

Ask Him to show you the world through His eyes. Ask how

you might join Him, how you might fit into that world as His hands, His feet, His voice.

Contemplatio

The fourth and final movement is the *contemplatio*, or contemplation.

This step is about sitting silently in the presence of God and about the reorientation of self toward Him. Toward His beauty.

This is not meditation; it is not reflection. This is resting. Stillness with God.

Let your body learn the joy of communion. In these silent moments, in this sacred time, God's truth will take root.

And that's it. That's the final step.

This practice can take five minutes, or it can take fifty. Linger as long as you need. The goal of *Lectio Divina* is transformation, not completion. The aim is union, not checking something off a list. The hope is to become like Jesus, to behold Him, and be transformed by Him. To know, not by fact, but by communion.

THE WORLD IS CHARGED WITH THE GRANDEUR OF GOD.

GERARD MANLEY HOPKINS[2]

VISIO DIVINA

In a similar way to *Lectio Divina*, we can use *Visio Divina*, or Divine Seeing, as a practice, a way to be transformed by the truth, goodness, and beauty of Christ.

From frescoes in Roman catacombs to stained-glass scenes in cathedrals, the Church has always used art as a means of orienting our hearts and minds, our souls and bodies, toward union with God. As a way of contemplation. Statues, icons, paintings, symphonies—each a kind of sacred language used to depict the reality of God. Some ancient icons depict entire scriptural themes, layered images that tell a theological story in a single moment.

For example, the icon of the Resurrection has motifs and concepts gathered and tied together forming a cohesive visual narrative. Christ stands at the center, resurrected, reaching to grab the wrists of Adam and Eve, pulling them, rescuing them from their tombs. At His left are David and Solomon, and at His right are Moses, Abel, and other prophets. Beneath His feet are the shattered gates of hell; the broken lock and key, which once held tight, are scattered beside them. And further below, a buried skeletal figure, bound and chained, lies in defeat.

This is visual theology—presented to us all at once—not over paragraphs and pages but as a single, sacred image. And it is an invitation to behold the message, to gaze into the depths of beauty and truth it contains.

This is the essence of *Visio Divina*—four slow and meditative movements aimed at unity, a way to behold and be transformed.

Begin in silence as preparation.

Gazing

The first movement is *gazing.*

It is not looking, scanning, glancing. Gazing is intentional; it is like listening with your eyes. And it is also an act of translation—learning the language of the artist and how that message relates to the truth, goodness, and beauty of God.

Gaze at the piece of art. Take it in slowly. Notice the colors and the contrasts, the proportions and the patterns. The unity, the harmony, the integrity. Look at the symbols and themes and subtleties. What is emphasized? What is hidden? Familiarize yourself with the piece.

Consideration

The second movement is *consideration.*

Ask questions.

What biblical or spiritual text is this piece about? What is being communicated? What are the symbols seeking to portray? Are there artistic themes? Narratives? Hierarchies? Ask what sticks out to you and why. How does this image meet you and speak into your life?

Begin to consider the *message* of the piece and how each aspect of it is communicating to you.

Contemplation

The third movement is *contemplation.*

Contemplation, here, is very similar to *Lectio Divina.* It is a silence before the presence of God, reflecting on the ways He has spoken to you and revealed His truth to you.

Let what you have seen become what you ponder before the Lord.

Maybe you see a fresh compassion in the face of Jesus in the Good Shepherd icon. And maybe this brings you a unique comfort in a time of suffering—maybe just as Jesus carries the weak lamb, you can see that He, too, carries you.

Maybe the broken gates of hell stir a longing for freedom. Freedom from whatever enslaves us.

This *contemplation* is an act of gratitude, rooted in reflection. It is nearness with our Creator.

Participation

The final movement of *Visio Divina* is *participation.*

Art will not leave us unmoved. This final moment is your life: the truth of beauty finding expression in your living and loving.

How will this art transform the way in which you move through the world?

Ponder what a life renewed by beauty might look like. Let this reflection stir up your heart and soul, your deepest affections, and then, after a closing prayer, embody the truth you have just seen.

Art has the extraordinary ability to *bypass* our usual mental gates and guards. Art doesn't speak primarily to the mind—art speaks soul to soul. It is a back door to the human heart.

In his Letter to Artists, Pope John Paul II wrote:

> Even beyond its typically religious expressions, true art has a close affinity with the world of faith, so that, even in situations where culture and the Church are far apart, art remains a kind of bridge to religious experience.[3]

Whether we participate in art through word or image, our goal is the same: to behold Christ. We want to see Him as He is, and we desire to be transformed. We want to breathe in His beauty and have Him sustain our lives. Our intention is to offer our whole selves, to offer our time and our effort and our focus, and to center who we are on Him. We are asking for eyes to see and ears to hear. Through this time, and by His grace, we will reteach ourselves how to see and how to hear—how to be seen and how to be heard. We see most clearly when we behold the living God. We hear most clearly when we listen to Him. And this is how we are transformed.

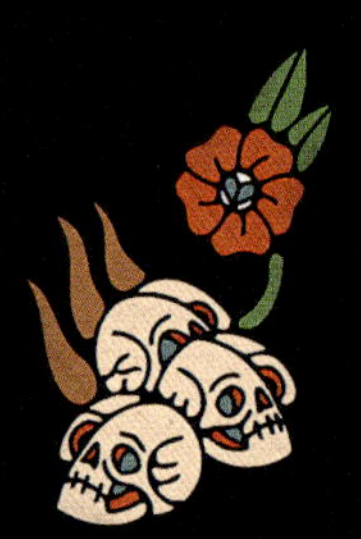

INTO THE WILDERNESS

HOW TO READ THIS BOOK

These two practices, *Lectio Divina* and *Visio Divina*, form the framework for approaching the Nicene Creed. I have divided the Creed into twenty phrases, and we will spend two days reflecting on each phrase.

The first day will be a *Lectio*-style reading of the phrase, with some reflections and questions to begin a time of quiet prayer. The second day will be a *Visio*-style reflection of that same phrase, using my art as a means for meditation. A caveat: I am no master among the great artists of history. I do not claim to create new icons or frescoes. All I can do is offer glimpses—a few frames of what God has allowed me to see. That is all art is: the gift of seeing with new eyes.

After those two days, we will move to the next phrase of the Creed and spend two days there—and so on, for forty days.

Why forty days? In Scripture, we come across time periods, either days or years, marked by the number forty. Rain poured down for forty days and forty nights while Noah and his family rode the ark safely over the flood. Moses fled to the wilderness of Midian for forty years after he killed the Egyptian, and he also interceded for Israel for forty days, begging God to spare them. Elijah ate a meal that satiated him for forty days.

And then there are times of testing and transformation: the Israelites wandering the wilderness for forty years before entering the promised land. Jesus, our Lord, fasting in the wilderness for forty days, confronting the devil, and emerging victorious. These are times of remaking, and they are times of preparation for all that is to come.

And many throughout Christian history have followed this same structure: celebrating Eastertide, Christmastide, and Lent, a forty-day fast in preparation for the Passion and the resurrection of Jesus.

And this is *why* the forty days matter. This book is a journey out into the wilderness, a time of transformation and preparation, a time to confront ourselves and our Enemy, a time to follow the truth and to emerge *more* like Christ.

I do not know what awaits you on this forty-day journey,

but I do promise you that the clean sea breeze of God will rush through you as you reflect on this Creed. I promise that you will smell ancient air, and you will feel the immanence of the King.

And you will find yourself remade in His presence.

O Lord, who, at the third hour, sent down your Holy Spirit on the apostles,

Do not take Him from us, O Good One, but renew Him in us, who pray to You.

Create in me a clean heart, O God, and put a new and constant spirit within me.

O Lord, who, at the third hour, sent down your Holy Spirit on the apostles,

Do not take Him from us, O Good One, but renew Him in us who pray to you.

Cast me not from your presence, and do not deprive me of your Holy Spirit.

O Lord, who, at the third hour, sent down your Holy Spirit on the apostles,

Do not take Him from us, O Good One, but renew Him in us who pray to you.

Glory to the Father, and to the Son, and to the Holy Spirit,
Now and ever and to the ages of ages.
Amen.[1]

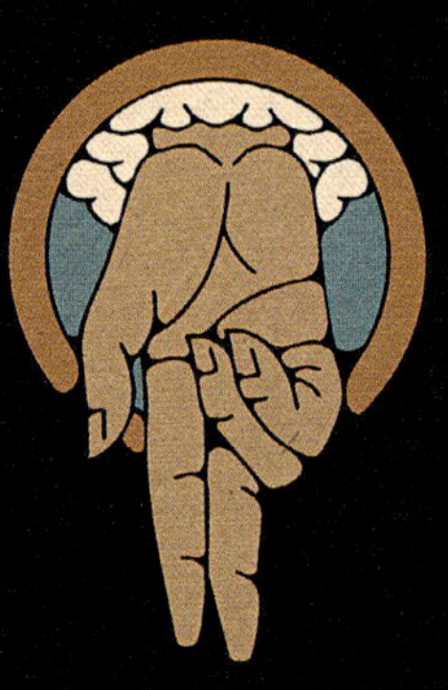

WE BELIEVE IN ONE GOD,
FATHER ALMIGHTY . . .

DAY 1

We.

Not alone, and not only here, and not only now.

We stand, united, in a long line of those who confess the *one* God. A line that stretches back through the corridors of history, back to the saints of old. Their mouths uttered these same words. Their voices, united, still echo through the ages. We join with them. And this reality we confess is faith in *one* God.

One in essence. God unified, harmonious.

This confession is not merely words but an embodiment of His reality, a reflection of His unity. He is one, and so, too, is our proclamation.

The Nicene Creed follows a Trinitarian structure. God exists in three persons—the Father, the Son, and the Holy Spirit—each fully God, sharing in *one* divine essence. *Essence* is just another way of saying *nature* or *being*. Three distinct persons, each fully and equally sharing the divine essence.

Our confession begins with God the Father. God reveals Himself to us primarily as Father, and the Father is the foundation of the Godhead. The Father is the sole cause of everything: without beginning, without end, everlasting, uncreated, sovereign, good, loving, patient, kind.

Father is a personal word. God, our Father, is not simply the highest being or the prime mover, not simply some immaterial concept. He is the Father of all; this is relational, a communion. This is the beauty: God desires to reveal Himself to us and to be known as love itself. Not far off. Not disinterested. Not estranged. But near. Compassionate. Engaged. A Father full of love.

Athanasius said that "God is good—or rather, of all goodness He is the Fountainhead."[1]

He is the Father of creation, and when Jesus, God's only begotten Son, teaches us to pray, He tells us to use that familial term: *our Father.* We are sons and daughters of God. We are called to participate in this love, to live in harmony with the heart of our Father, in union with Him in our living and moving and being.

Our Father is *Almighty.*

He is the true ruler of all things. His reign cannot be frustrated or upended or overturned. His authority has no end. He does not command the cosmos by force or temper but with benevolence, mercy, strength, and justice.

We confess one God, the Father Almighty.

REFLECT AND MEDITATE

Reflect upon how this confession unites you with brothers and sisters across time, how we might be a living echo of God's unity.

Consider what it means for God to be our Father—from whom all fatherhood takes its name (Ephesians 3:14–15). Your Father delights in you—you are a son, a daughter, to Him. His love for you isn't forced or fake; it's true and deep. His delight in you is good, and His desire is that, as Jesus prayed, you would be in unity with the "Fountainhead of goodness."

Meditate upon the might of God, about how His cosmos will, one day, be a full and complete reflection of who He is and how you might play a part in this great work.

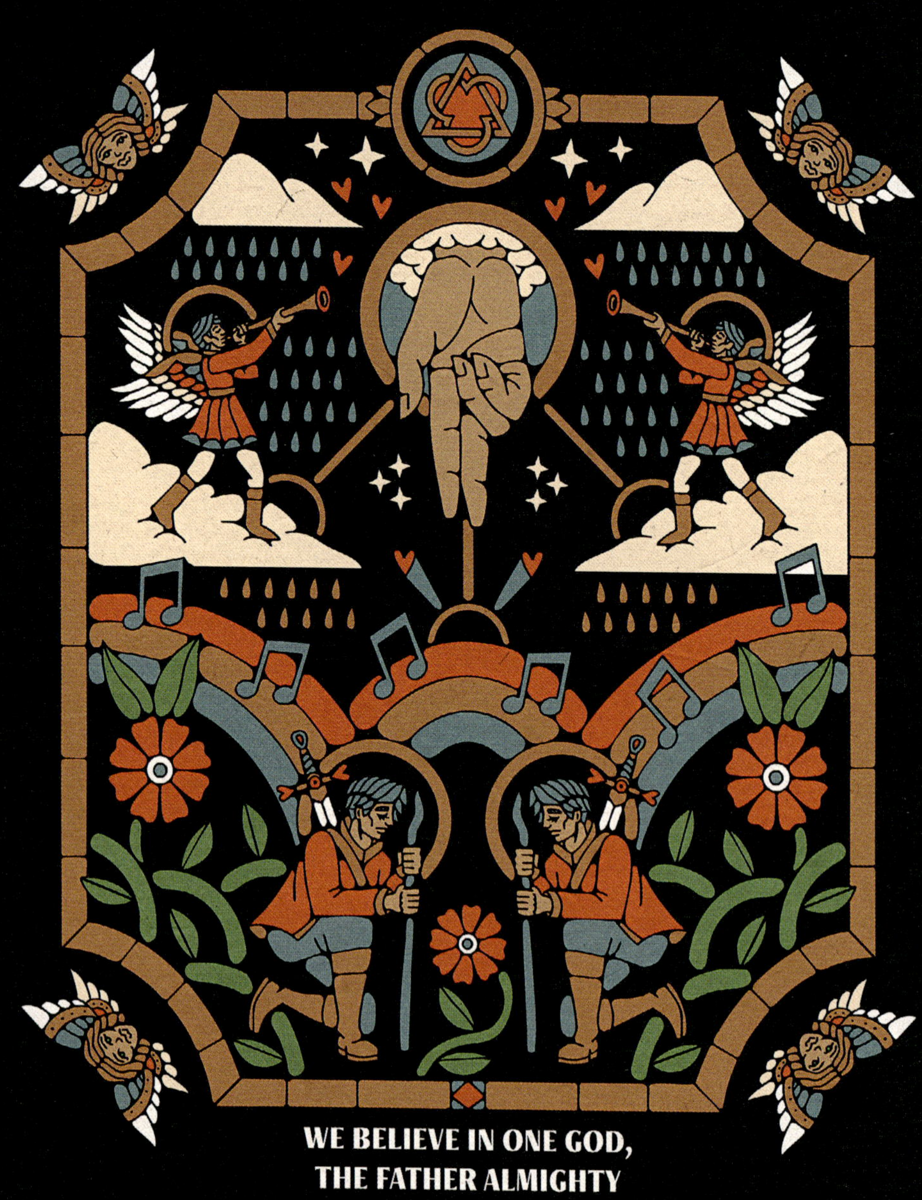

WE BELIEVE IN ONE GOD,
THE FATHER ALMIGHTY

DAY 2

Within this first phrase of the Nicene Creed is an embedded mystery. We believe in *one God*—a Trinity. This concept, one God in three Persons, is unknowable in its fullness. God is infinite, and we are finite. But this mystery is not a deterrent. It is an invitation into all the goodness of God, for within this triune mystery lies the fullness of God.

And this mystery is personal, close and near. We can feel His presence, and we can know Him. He is as "narrow as the universe,"[1] closer than wide spaces, nearer than our own self. This is an echo of the paradox Paul prays in Ephesians 3:18–19, to comprehend the incomprehensible, and "to know the love of Christ which passes knowledge; that you may be filled with all the fullness of God" (NKJV).

To know the unknowable. To be filled with the uncontainable.

Framing the image are the angels at the four corners of the world. This is symbolic, a way to show that the entirety of the cosmos is in view. God's voice thunders, and it is sent forth under heaven, and His light goes to the ends of the earth (Job 37:2–3).

Embedded in the frame of the cosmos is a symbol for the

Trinity: the Father, the Son, and the Spirit, sharing one divine essence.

Below we see the hand of blessing, the Father Himself reaching down in love over His creation, reaching down because He is highest of all.

Kneeling at the bottom of the image are the saints and pilgrims, walking sticks in their hands and swords on their backs, symbols of the sojourn into eternity and a commitment to the Word of God. These saints worship together, bowing before the Father Almighty.

Around them is the untamed cosmos, which humanity has been commissioned to till into Eden. The wilderness reveals that these saints, and we with them, make confession between the times. Before the end of all things. Before all is made new.

Beams of light flow from the Father's hands, and Creation echoes with His song. This is an allusion to both J. R. R. Tolkien and C. S. Lewis, who, in their respective creation accounts, depict the divine as singing all things into existence.[2] Creation is no machine—it is a symphony.

Angels worship in the skies above, the same angels who cry out ceaselessly in worship of the Father Almighty. And all around them is divine love, which rains down upon the earth, feeding it, for all creation is nourished by divine love.

REFLECT AND MEDITATE

Take a moment to reflect upon the hierarchy of this image. Think about how and why each aspect finds its respective place.

Consider the layered truths depicted—the themes and passages—and how they overlap and expand upon each other. How do they fill out the confession of one God, the Father Almighty?

Meditate on what it means to be a confessor "between the times." How might you bring the goodness of God to the wilderness around you?

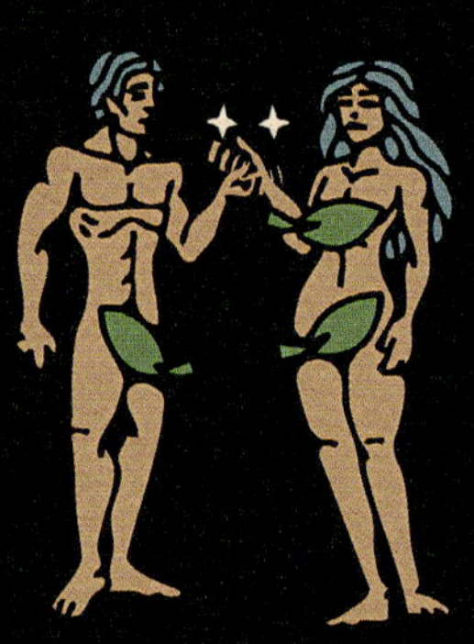

. . . CREATOR OF HEAVEN AND EARTH,
OF ALL THINGS VISIBLE AND INVISIBLE.

DAY 3

The Father Almighty displays His power in creation. He is the source of all that has been made, everything, the entire cosmos, from the very top to the very bottom. The Creed echoes with the same language of the first words of the Scriptures: "In the beginning God created the heavens and the earth" (Genesis 1:1 NKJV).

And in these words, we can breathe in that ancient air.

Creation reverberates with the glory of God. It is imprinted with His love and power, with His mystery and His immanence. It is a reflection, in some capacity, of who He is. The Father rules over this creation, and He creates all things by love, through love, and for love, and because of this, all creation invites us back to Him.

Creation is not accidental, not a mistake. It is a work of intentional purpose, a production of infinite joy. G. K. Chesterton captures this infinite joy in his book *Orthodoxy*:

> But perhaps God is strong enough to exult in monotony. It is possible that God says every morning, "Do it again" to the sun; and every evening, "Do it again" to the moon. It may not be automatic necessity that makes all daisies alike; it may be that God makes every daisy separately, but has never got tired of making

them. It may be that He has the eternal appetite of infancy; for we have sinned and grown old, and our Father is younger than we.[1]

Perhaps all of creation is still *being made*, even now—day after day—by our Father, in acts of infinite joy. And perhaps the next time you see a leaf or cloud or sunset, you will be able to hear echoes of His pleasure.

Creation is also a reflection of the generosity of God, a display of His delight to bestow good gifts upon His children. Mountains and rivers and the kaleidoscope of colors at dusk, great fish and lions and butterflies, tulips and redwoods and cherry blossoms, the rain that feeds our earth, the fires that warm our homes and cook our food—each a gift of beauty, a reflection of His order, His happiness, His care, and His goodness.

Our Father is the maker of all things. This language speaks of *realms*: God is the creator of more than matter, more than the physical world. In Colossians 1:16, we see that He is also the maker of all spiritual things, the invisible, angels (including those who fell), and souls.

This is a layered Trinitarian understanding of the Godhead. The Father, through the Son, by the Spirit, maker of all things visible and invisible.

God is not a part of the *all things*. He is not created, nor is He some manifestation of the universe, as the pantheists believe. No, our Father's glory and majesty are seated above the heavens and the earth.

REFLECT AND MEDITATE

Reflect on how creation is an imprint of God, an echo of His beauty and generosity. Think of those things in creation that stir up joy and love within you. Consider them as gifts, and meditate on how they reflect the Person of God.

Meditate upon the "Father who is younger than we." The God who never tires of beauty or grows bored of "monotony." Meditate upon the Father who never wearies of sunrise, who delights in each day as if it were the first one.

Consider His joy, and ponder what it might take to become as a child and enjoy His beauty.

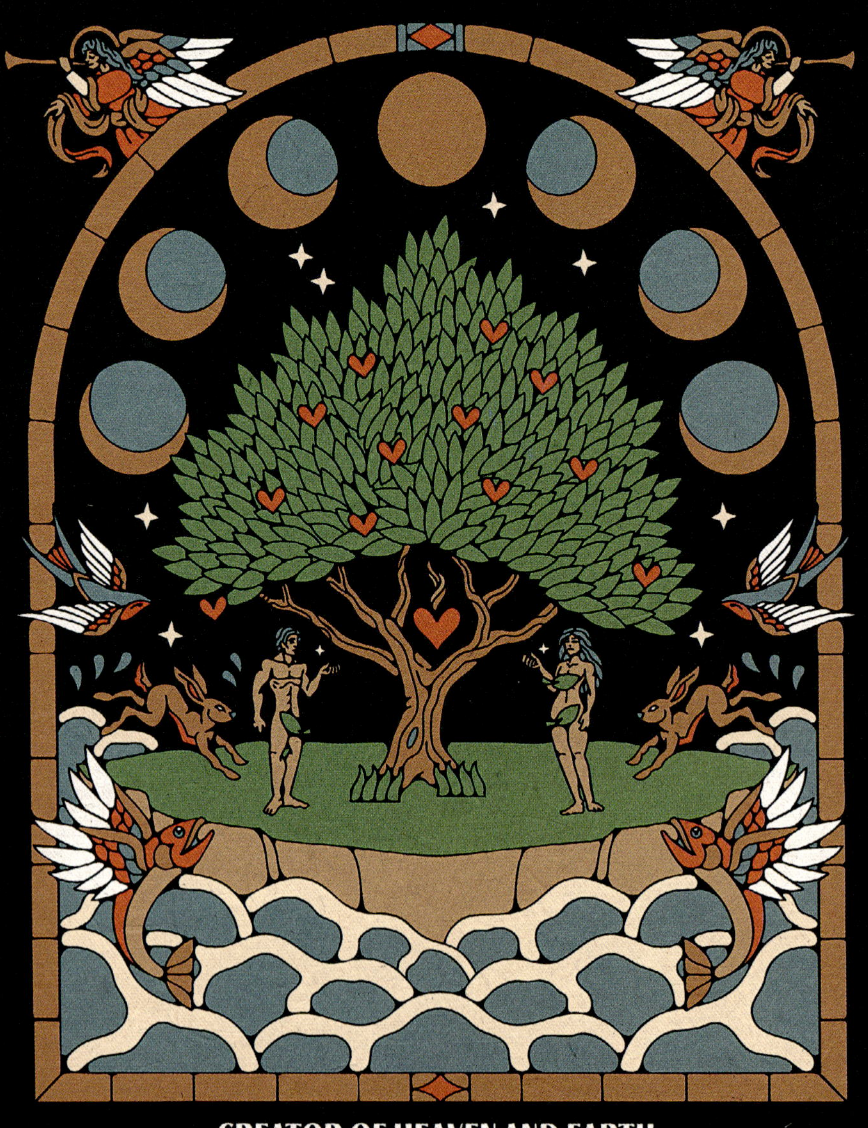

CREATOR OF HEAVEN AND EARTH,
OF ALL THINGS VISIBLE AND INVISIBLE.

DAY 4

This piece takes the shape of a stained-glass window, providing a moment for us to look through it and *see* creation with fresh eyes. The shape also reflects an ancient understanding of the cosmos—the land sat upon the waters, held up by the foundations of the earth, enclosed by a great dome, and a firmament, which separated the heavens from the earth. Above the dome is the realm of the invisible creatures, the domain of spiritual beings.

At the top of the dome, or arched window, is a symbol for God the Father, who is above the heavens and the earth. And beside Him are angelic beings, those which are *invisible*, and they are worshipping, singing along with the song of creation.

Within the window, we see the phases of the day, seven of them, representing the days of creation found in Genesis. We see light made, separate from darkness. We see the sky separated from the waters and the waters separated from the land.

And then we see the further generosity of God in filling these spaces with all good things: the sun and moon and stars to govern day and night. We see creatures that will fill the seas to teeming, and we see vegetation and animals on land. And we see, in the doves, an echo of the Spirit hovering over the waters.

Adam and Eve are there, too, the crown of creation, images of God Himself, intended to be the keepers of Eden. They are to subdue the whole earth, to be fruitful, and to take this garden and multiply it, bringing order to the chaos. They are standing in the center of the land, beneath the Tree of Life. This tree bears good fruit, pleasant for eating, and each fruit is in the shape of a heart, symbolizing that we feast and survive on the loving life of God.

And Adam and Eve are naked, and they have no shame.

REFLECT AND MEDITATE

Reflect upon the structure of the image, of the order of things. Consider how this structure of creation reflects the nature of God.

All of humanity is made as an image of God. Take time to consider what it would mean for you to multiply Eden, to bring God's good order to the world around you.

Consider what it means to feast upon the loving life of God and what it means to be naked and unashamed before Him and His creation.

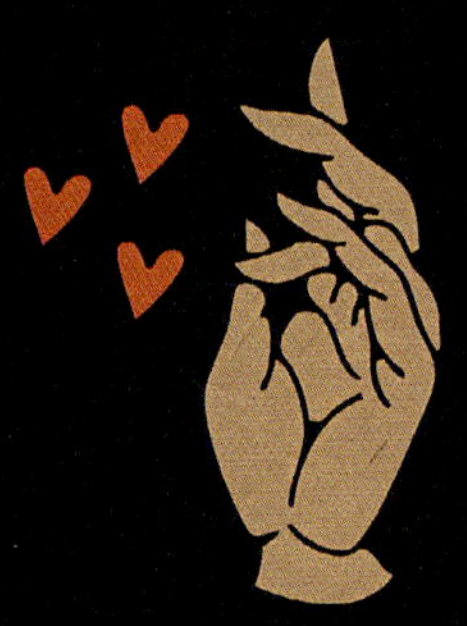

**WE BELIEVE IN ONE LORD JESUS CHRIST,
THE ONLY-BEGOTTEN SON OF GOD,
BEGOTTEN OF THE FATHER BEFORE ALL AGES . . .**

DAY 5

The Nicene Creed now moves to the second person of the *one God*—the person of the Lord Jesus Christ. Two things are happening at once in this phrase. First, we experience an echo of the earlier phrase "We believe in one God," a poetic telegraphing of the divinity of the Son. Second, we find the use of the word *Lord*, which in the New Testament is a title given to Jesus. In the Septuagint (the Greek translation of the Old Testament), *Lord* is the word used for the divine name *Yahweh*—a theological telegraphing of the divinity of the Son.

This one Lord Jesus Christ is of the same essence of God the Father.

This phrase "Lord Jesus Christ" speaks about kingship and authority. It closely parallels the idea of "Father Almighty." Jesus is the Lord. Jesus is the King. Jesus has all authority. But there can only be one God. And there can only be one divine name. To confess Christ as Lord is to confess Him as the God of Abraham, Isaac, and Jacob. And to bow before Jesus and worship Him as Lord is to worship the triune God.

Also carried in these phrases are the concepts of salvation and rescue. The name *Jesus* means "Yahweh saves." God will set His people free, conjuring up images of the exodus, and Jesus is ushering in a new exodus. The word *Christ* is not a name; it's a title, meaning "anointed one" or "messiah." And this Jesus, who we confess, is the anointed King who will save His people from their greatest enemies of sin and death. He will rescue humanity from a bondage that has enslaved us since we first ate of the fruit. The new exodus.

And Jesus is the only *begotten* Son of God. This is His identity. This Son is the Word of God, and He is full of grace and truth. *Begetting* is an old word, and in the King James Bible I read growing up, there were lists of *begats*, like in Genesis 11. These described a lineage, a son from a source. The Creed uses this language to show us that Jesus is a Son by nature, the *only begotten* Son of God. The only Son by nature and essence.

This Son reveals the Father and is, in fact, a true icon and image of the Father. Jesus said that if we have seen the Son, we have seen the Father. Christ "is the image of the invisible God, the firstborn of every creature" (Colossians 1:15 KJV). This Son is God.

The Lord Jesus Christ shares the same divine essence of the Father, but the Son is *begotten* of the Father. This is part of the mystery of the Trinity—the Son was not created, and there is not a time before the Son existed, but He is *born of God*. He originates from the Source. This is not a kind of subordination, as the Creed will go on to clarify. He is a Son before all ages, coeternal, and sharing in the divine essence.

REFLECT AND MEDITATE

Consider how the New Testament and the Creed use the same word for the divine name to describe Jesus: the Christ.

Reflect on what it means that "He will save His people from their sins" (Matthew 1:21 NKJV*) in light of this reality.*

Meditate on this Son of God, who is the image of the invisible God, and consider what the Christ in the Gospels reveals about God the Father in the whole story of Scripture.

And as 1 John 3:1 reminds us, behold what manner of love has been shown to us, that we might be called sons and daughters of God—not by nature but by rescue and desire.

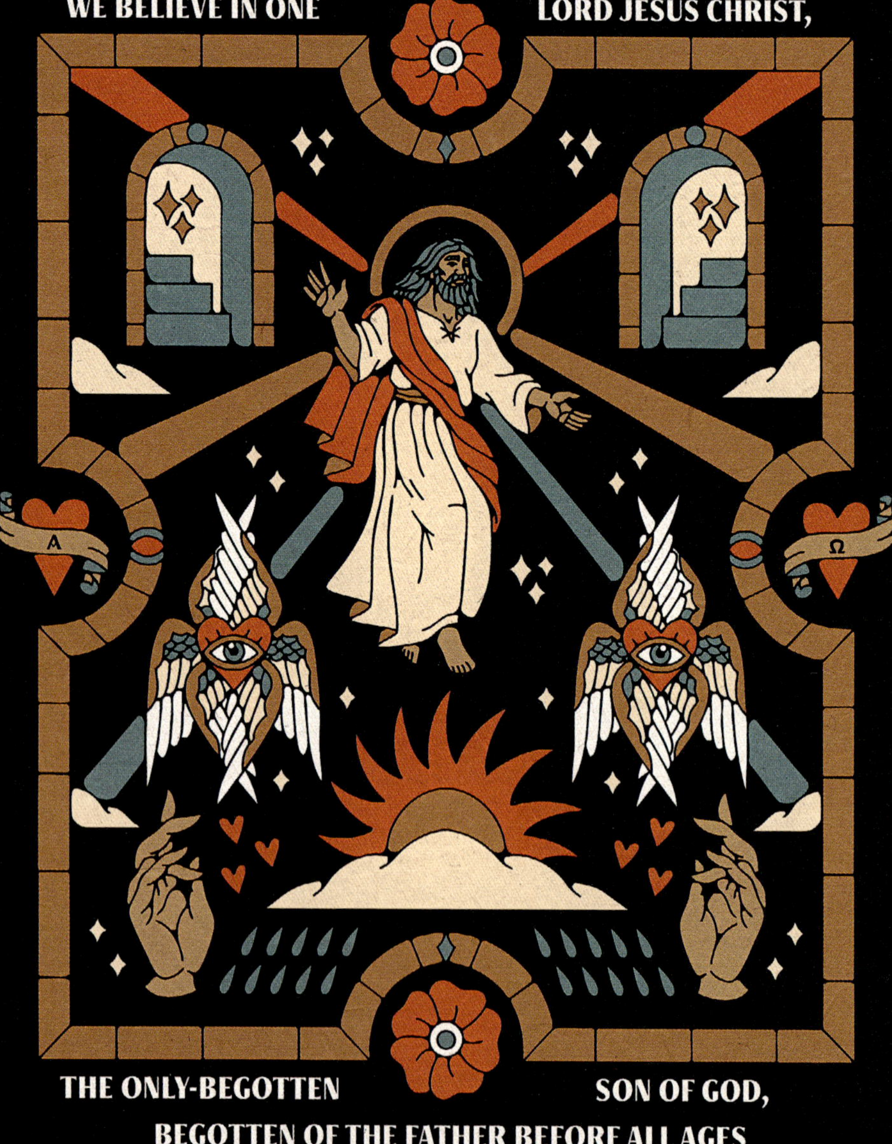
WE BELIEVE IN ONE
LORD JESUS CHRIST,
A
Ω
THE ONLY-BEGOTTEN
SON OF GOD,
BEGOTTEN OF THE FATHER BEFORE ALL AGES

DAY 6

Shining in the center of this piece is the preincarnate Christ. Shining in the center of this piece is the preincarnate Christ, a theophany. *Theophanies* are manifestations of God in a tangible form, sometimes as a burning bush, sometimes as a pillar of fire or smoke, often as the "angel of the LORD" (Genesis 16:7, 13; Exodus 3:2–6). This angel of the Lord is Christ before His incarnation. In Judges 13, for example, when Manoah and his wife said, "We have seen God!" (v. 22 NKJV), it was the preincarnate Jesus they saw, since no one can see the Father and live (Exodus 33:20). This is revelation made visible.

In this piece, the Lord Jesus Christ is crowned as King and is shining with the same glorious light that we saw in the Father's hand of blessing—denoting that Father and Son are both God, sharing the same divine essence. Framing Him above are stairways to heaven, a riff on Jacob's Ladder, a bridge between heaven and earth. Jesus, Yahweh, saves; the Messiah is the bridge by which we enter the heavens.

Below the Lord and framing Him on either side are seraphim. This references John 12:41, in which John said that Jesus is the one pictured in Isaiah 6:1–3:

> I saw also the LORD sitting upon a throne, high and
> lifted up, and his train filled the temple. Above

> it stood the seraphims. . . . And one cried unto another, and said, Holy, holy, holy, is the LORD of hosts: the whole earth is full of his glory. (KJV)

Jesus is worshipped as the Lord of hosts, of those visible and invisible, who are portrayed in the stars around the cosmos. The whole earth, the whole cosmos, is His temple. And His temple is filled with His glory, with the weight of His beauty.

Below the feet of Jesus is the sun, symbolizing how Jesus is the true Son of glory, that He is the true Light of the world, that those who follow Him and His path will never be in darkness but will walk in His marvelous light.

The hands that frame the bottom of the artwork are used in Christian art as a symbol of blessing; the fingers spell out *ICXC*, a Greek abbreviation of Jesus Christ, the name above every name. Further, the three fingers used to spell the *I* and the *X* represent the Trinity: Father, Son, and Spirit. And the thumb and the ring finger touching shows the union of the human and divine natures in God the Son.

This piece is framed by poppies at the top and bottom, symbols of the life of Christ, as poppies can continue to bloom even after times of barrenness. And to the left and the right are hearts and banners with the symbols *alpha* and *omega*, showing that Jesus is God, beginning and end, before all ages.

REFLECT AND MEDITATE

This piece is intended to put together the aspects contained within the titles and names in this phrase of the Creed. The Lord, the Savior, the King. Take time to reflect on these images.

Reflect on what it means for Jesus to be true Light, that outside of His way is darkness, and consider the ways in which you might follow Him.

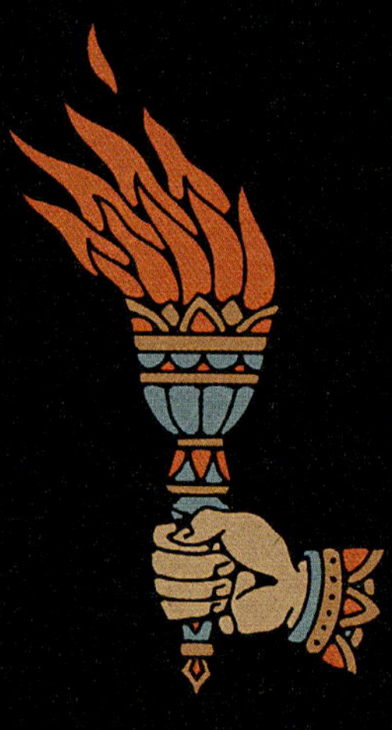

. . . LIGHT OF LIGHT,
TRUE GOD OF TRUE GOD,
BEGOTTEN, NOT CREATED,
OF ONE ESSENCE WITH THE FATHER . . .

DAY 7

Jesus, who is the Lord, is Light of Light. Just as the sun is never without light, so, too, is God the Father never without the Son. They both exist from all eternity. Just as we cannot touch the sun, lest we be consumed by its heat and power, so, too, we cannot touch the Father. We can live in the rays of the sun. So, too, can we live in the bright glory of the Son's light.

We are reminded again that the Son is *from* the Father, God *of* God, Light *of* Light. We can behold His glory, and by His light, we can understand our Father Almighty. The light of the Son is our life, and by tracing those divine beams back to the Source, we can know our Father, who is in heaven.

Jesus is not simply *like* the Father, not simply an emissary of the Father sent in some sort of subordinating assignment. Jesus is also True God, as the Father is True God. He was *begotten*, but He was not made, not crafted out of material substances—Jesus is uncreated. He has all the essential attributes of God because He shares in the divine essence. He is *con*substantial with the Father. This phrase is famous in its defense against Arianism—the heresy that denied the full divinity of Jesus—and not only defends the deity of Christ but asserts that in God there is one love, one grace, one power, and one will. Jesus reveals this to us; He makes that which is invisible visible. In the person of Christ, God is revealed, made manifest to us, in ways we can understand. In ways we touch and see and feel.

There was this moment in the Gospels, out in the wilderness, up on Mount Tabor with Peter, James, and John, when Jesus was transfigured. When His face shined like the sun, when His garments were white, and when Moses and Elijah appeared. These two, Moses and Elijah, represented the Law and the prophets. They represented the living and the dead, as Elijah had been taken up into heaven, while Moses tasted death. And they both had visions of God—they saw the divine light. Peter wanted to remain there, in that light, in that glory, in that life. And then the bright cloud overwhelmed them, and the voice of the Father spoke out: "This is My beloved Son, with whom I am well pleased; listen to Him!" (Matthew 17:5 NASB).

And what did Jesus say elsewhere in the Gospels? Jesus said that He is the Light of the World and that we may become children of the light—and that light is the beauty and majesty and glory of the triune God. And Jesus also invites us to be the light of the world, to reflect His divine rays out into the darkness. He said a time is coming when we will live in the light forever, but for now, we are cities on a hill, places of refuge, shining out to a lost and broken world.

REFLECT AND MEDITATE

Reflect upon the living unity between Father and Son—that they have always existed together in harmony and love. And consider that the Son invites us to participate in this harmony so that we may be one with God, as He is.

Consider how Jesus translates to us the light of the glory of the Father and that, by knowing Jesus and seeing Him, we can know the Father and be known by Him.

Imagine yourself on the Mount of Transfiguration, confronted with the true and shining King, and try to hear afresh the words of the Father: "This is My beloved Son, with whom I am well pleased; listen to Him!" In what ways must you listen to Jesus?

LIGHT FROM LIGHT, TRUE GOD OF TRUE GOD,

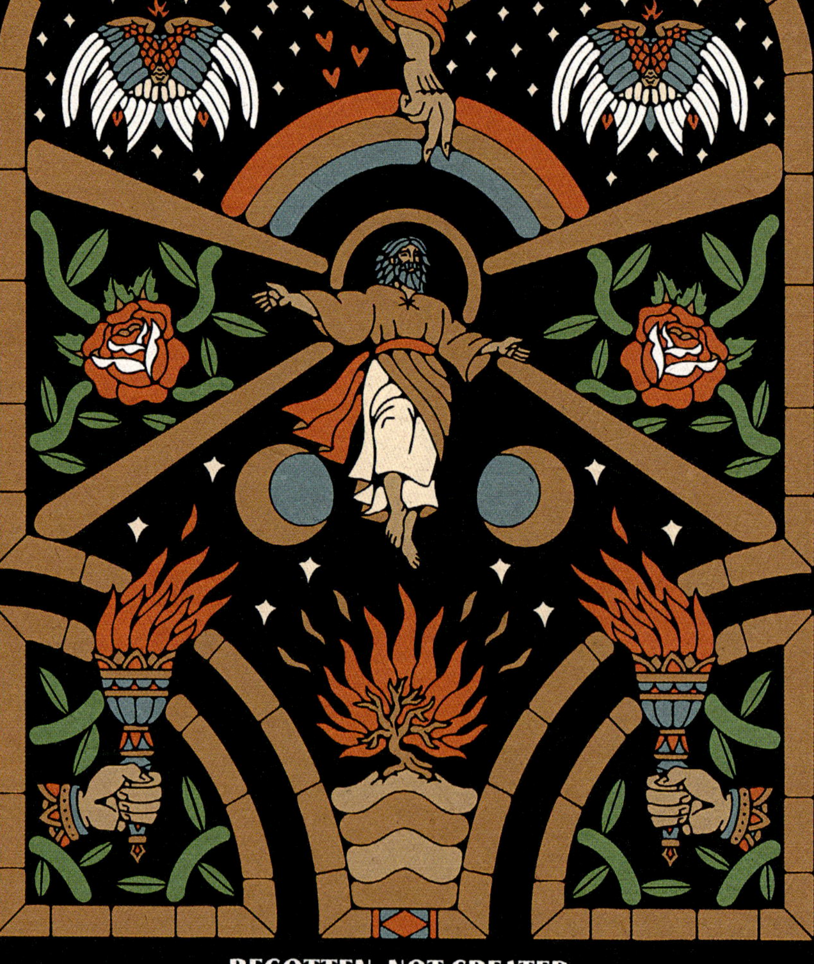

BEGOTTEN, NOT CREATED,

DAY 8

In this piece, Christ is reaching out from atop the mountain, transfigured—shining with bright and radiant glory that reaches out into the heavens and the earth. The Father's hand of blessing is an echo of the transfiguration in Matthew 17; the Father blesses the Son, and with the Son He is well pleased.

Between the Father and the Son is light, love, and a rainbow. The light is a symbol of *Light of Light*. The hearts are a symbol of the intra-Trinitarian love, the mutual love that the Father and the Son have for each other. The rainbow is a symbol of their triune glory: "Like the appearance of a rainbow in a cloud on a rainy day, so was the appearance of the brightness all around it. This was the appearance of the likeness of the glory of the LORD" (Ezekiel 1:28 NKJV).

In the heavens above are seraphim who must cover their eyes, for they, too, cannot behold the full glory of God. Framing Jesus on His left and right are flourishing roses; it is by the light of God that we are nourished and fed and have our life.

Below Jesus are two moons, one representing light that shines out into the darkness, and the other reminding that God will protect His own (Psalm 121:6).

On the ground is the burning bush, the symbol of Yahweh's bright burning, of sacred ground, of immanence. The contrast drawn here is that this light does not consume, and Jesus' light, too, does not consume us.

Finally, there is a split in the piece. At the bottom are two hands, each holding out a torch in the wilderness. This represents those of us who follow Christ. We do not have the fullness of divine light by nature. We are creatures, yet we still share this light—shining it into the darkness, guiding others toward the light and life of Jesus.

REFLECT AND MEDITATE

Ponder all that the Father and the Son share: light, love, life, and anything else God brings to mind. Think about how the Son reveals this, even now, in your life.

Think about what it means for the light of Christ to be a rainbow on a rainy day, how God's glory can transform even the greatest of storms.

Imagine yourself on that hallowed ground, before the burning light of God. Imagine what it would feel like to see and sense His glory. Take those feelings and let them fuel your torch, bringing His light to those who remain in darkness.

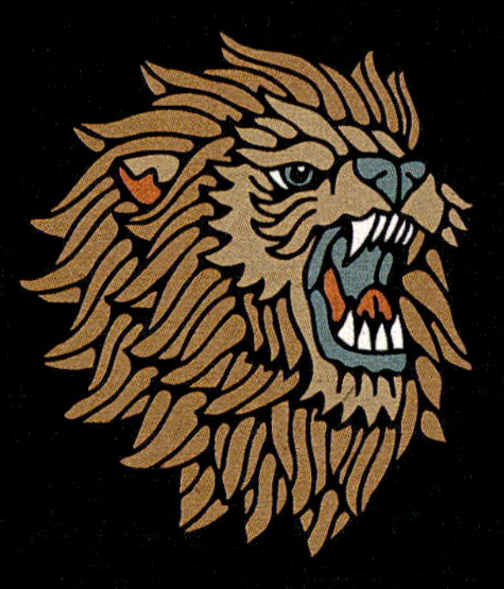

. . . THROUGH WHOM ALL THINGS WERE MADE.

DAY 9

In this phrase, the Nicene Creed quotes from John 1: "All things were made by him; and without him was not any thing made that was made" (v. 3 KJV). This passage also speaks of the Son as the Word of God, who was with God in the beginning, and that this Word was and is truly God. The phrasing from John also echoes Genesis—"In the beginning"—which the Creed has already stated about the Father.

Creation is *by* the Father, *through* the Son. And this is what we, the Church, believe.

It is by the Word that God made the heavens and the earth, an echo of God speaking creation into existence, commanding chaos to find order. It is by this Word that all things were made. All of creation, all that is good, was made by Jesus. Even those beautiful things His creatures make, like children, or poems, or pottery—we make them because He made us, and creativity is hereditary, and He sustains us.

Creation reflects the glory of God, and yet it remains distinct from Him. When we say that creation is a reflection, we mean it as Maximus the Confessor taught: that creation is a kind of sacramental theophany—a visible sign that reveals invisible divine realities.[1]

Since this cosmos was made through the Word, everything good, true, and beautiful within it is patterned after Him. Winter always gives way to spring; trees burst forth with fruitful life; and after every dark night is a bright dawn.

Christ is the archetype for every good created thing—*good* as in the Genesis kind of good, as in "declared good." Everything we see that is good and true and beautiful has those characteristics because Jesus is their source. Those things we love? We love them because they were made by Him who is infinitely lovely.

REFLECT AND MEDITATE

Meditate upon the power of God: the power to command all things out of no things, the power to bring order to chaos, the power to make beauty manifest.

Consider the words God has spoken to you in this moment.

Take time to ponder your favorite part of creation: mountains or fruits, clouds or wind, ants or eagles or horses, the moon's cycles, the seasons, the sea. Reflect on how all these things echo Christ—the archetype of creation, the true source from whom all loveliness flows.

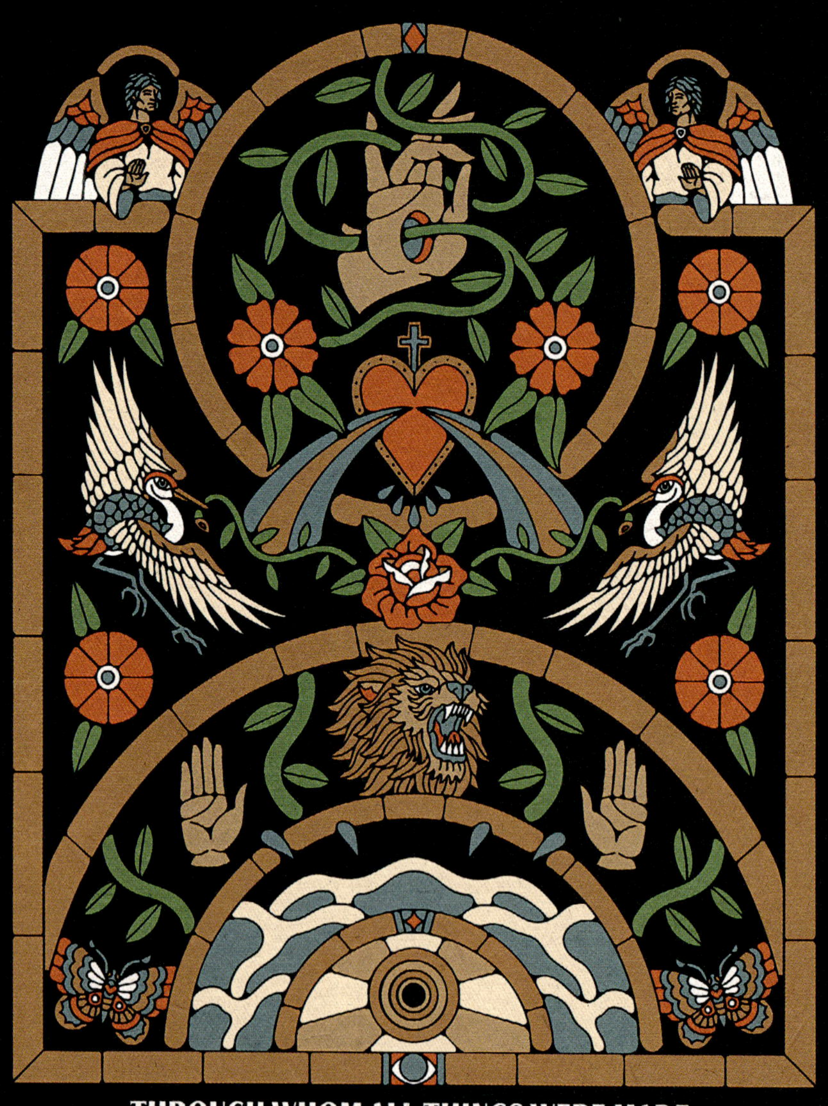

THROUGH WHOM ALL THINGS WERE MADE.

DAY 10

Christ's hand of blessing is framed with vines and flowers at the top of this canvas, a further symbol of the Trinity and also of the unity of the divine and human natures in Jesus. The flowers and the vines riff on the idea of remaining in Christ in order to bear much fruit; creation *remains* because it comes from and is sustained by Christ.

There are two cranes, their wings curving around this hand of blessing. These symbolize calling out to God for life and healing and restoration, as in Isaiah 38. Creation has been made good, but because of rebellion, not all in creation remains good. Some things exist in opposition to God and His goodness, requiring Christ's rescue. These cranes are holding on to a vine and flower, needing to remain in Christ. And there is a heart, from the hand of Christ, pouring down onto the cranes. This reveals to us that while all of creation groans for redemption, all things will, one day, be made new.

The concentric circles are reflections of the seven days of creation. They carry the idea that these seven days, and all of creation, make up the temple in which God reigns. His cosmos is His temple, and in His cosmos, He alone is King.

In these circles are aspects of creation that I personally delight in.

The late rays of dusk and the rolling tides of the sea.

The transforming beauty of a butterfly and human hands with which we touch the world around us.

A lion—fierce and majestic.

Any good created thing could be here, and perhaps you might take some extra time to imagine your favorite parts of creation in the hierarchy of this piece.

REFLECT AND MEDITATE

All creation remains in existence because of the grace and power of the Word. Reflect on the kindness of God to sustain all things and His grace to restore all things.

Imagine what creation made new will be like, how each and every thing you love is but a shadow of its true substance.

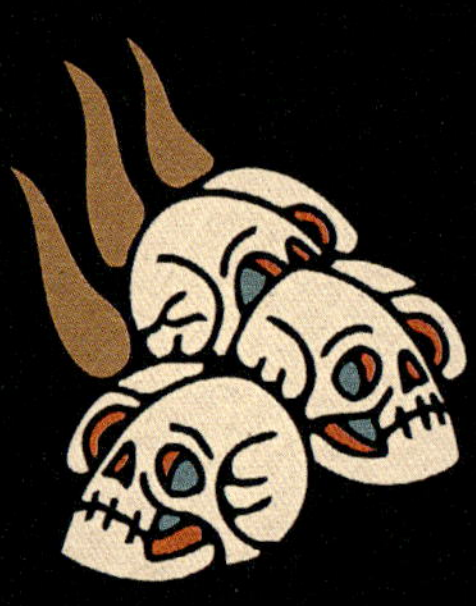

FOR US MEN AND FOR OUR SALVATION
HE CAME DOWN FROM HEAVEN,

DAY 11

And now the Creed mentions humanity.

Our free choices, our desire to rebel against God, and the image He intends us to reflect distanced us from His light and life. That is why "the wages of sin is death" (Romans 6:23 KJV)—because we have removed ourselves from the life of God.

Eden tells this story in Genesis 3: Humans were meant to feast on the Tree of Life and remain in the presence of God forever. But when they rebelled, they were cast out—cut off from life. And so, they would surely perish.

But the Lord Jesus, our Christ, of His own free choice, came down from heaven to make way the path of salvation, to reconcile God and man. The first step in this salvation plan is the *incarnation*: God in the flesh. Born in a stable, under the floor of the world, shaking the very foundations of the earth. The shadows of the Old Testament—the theophanies—were glimpses of Him. But this is the substance: God made manifest. This Christ, the Lord, came down from heaven and took on flesh.

He did this for our salvation, a perfect expression of the love the Father Almighty has for His children, the beams of glory that reflect the source.

Jesus came down from heaven, revealing His humility. He was previously seated with the Father, reigning and ruling over the cosmos. And then the Creator entered His creation. God became man. This incarnation is a full expression of God's love, generosity, and desire for reconciliation and salvation.

Salvation is the restoration of Eden, in fullness. The garden, in Eden, was the template for the cosmos, and humanity was intended to participate in the life of God and carry that beauty and goodness to the corners of the universe. We know the story—the rejection of God's ways and the loss of consuming His life—but salvation in Christ unites us with God again.

We will be restored to fellowship with God, reconciled, so as to walk with Him in the cool of the day, except here, we will be set free. Free to truly choose the good—to feast upon the life of God forever. Eden perfected.

REFLECT AND MEDITATE

Ponder all the ways you still reject the life of God. What might this rejection be doing to you, body and soul?

Reflect upon the kindness of God, who, for your sake, stepped down from His glorious throne to reconcile with you and offer you His life.

Imagine the life to come—when heaven meets earth. Consider how you might begin to participate in that fullness even today.

FOR US MEN AND FOR OUR SALVATION

DOMINUS ILLUMINATIO MEA

CAME DOWN FROM HEAVEN

DAY 12

At the very center of this image is Christ the King, reigning over His creation—and it is this King who humbles Himself and steps down, making His dwelling among us, full of grace and truth. Love motivated this descent; love drove the King from His throne, down to rescue His beloved.

At the top of the image are angels announcing this *coming down*. There are shepherds out in the wilderness, and appearing before them is a heavenly host proclaiming, "Glory to God in the highest, and on earth peace, goodwill toward men!" (Luke 2:14 NKJV).

These angels are rejoicing in the love of God, in the glory of God made manifest, who brings peace where once there was animosity and rebellion. Between this myriad of angels is a sacred heart—a symbol of the sacrificial love of Christ. The heart is pierced, as Christ was for us. The burning flames represent the purifying and transforming power of divine love, and the fire sparks out into all creation, for the whole cosmos will be redeemed.

Below is a representation of humanity, weeping, mourning in lonely exile, crying out for rescue. These two men hold a banner reading, *"Dominus illuminatio mea,"* or "The LORD is my light"

(Psalm 27:1 NKJV, as translated from the Vulgate, the Latin translation of the Bible). The two have broken and bleeding hearts. They cannot survive on their own, and between them lie the skulls of many who have been defeated by humanity's great enemy: death.

All at once, we can see the heavenly host announcing the coming King, the Messiah of humanity, coming down to rescue His lost and broken people from sin and death.

REFLECT AND MEDITATE

Reflect on the humility of Jesus the King. Consider how you might embody that same humility—giving yourself for the good of others.

Imagine the joy of the heavenly host, and place yourself in the scene. See the joyful celebration; hear the song of heaven.

Meditate on the state of humanity apart from the life of God. Ponder what it means for the light of heaven to be made manifest in such darkness.

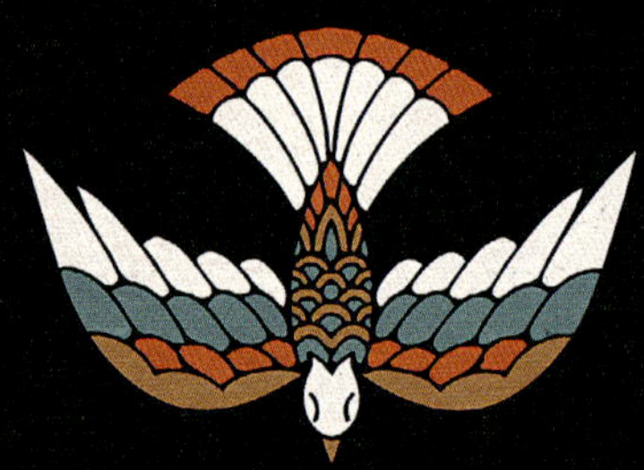

. . . AND WAS INCARNATE OF THE HOLY SPIRIT AND THE VIRGIN MARY AND BECAME MAN.

DAY 13

The incarnation is accomplished by the power of the Holy Spirit, and the divine nature of the Word is united to a human nature. This is vital to understanding the person of Jesus. Just as He is truly God *from* God, so, too, is He truly Man *from* man:

> But when the fulness of the time was come, God sent forth his Son, made of a woman, made under the law, to redeem them that were under the law, that we might receive the adoption of sons. (Galatians 4:4–5 KJV)

Jesus was not *fathered* as humans are. And still Jesus was born, as all humans are, of a woman. Jesus, the Son of God, passed through the birth canal of a woman. What is unique in the birth of God is that His mother, Mary, was a virgin. And this seems to be the substance of all those promised sons placed in barren wombs in the Old Testament, a gift of life by the Holy Spirit. It is by the power of the Holy Spirit that Mary bore a son, the true promised Son. Her cousin Elizabeth recognized this and called Mary the "mother of my Lord" (Luke 1:43 NKJV), or *Theotokos* in Greek. Mary bore God—gave birth to God—in the sense that Jesus is *God from God*. Contained within her womb was her uncontainable Creator.

Jesus took on a full human nature. He became like us, yet without sin, so that in Him we might defeat death. As Athanasius said, "God became man so that man might become God."[1] This doesn't mean that we become "uncreated" and eternal or that we merge with the divine essence. Rather, as the church fathers taught, this is the *mystery* of *theosis*. As 2 Peter 1:4 says, we are made "partakers of the divine nature" (KJV).

Through Christ we are restored to image Him as intended and to participate in Him and His divine life. We are to make manifest, in our small ways, the divine attributes: love, joy, peace. Or as C. S. Lewis simply put it, we are called to become "little Christs."[2]

In the incarnation, the body is sanctified, redeemed from its fallen state. Jesus is the true image of the Father, an exact representation of God embodied. Mary was the new ark of the covenant, carrying the Word within her. She was also the new Eve, the better Eve, who gave birth to the promised Son who would crush the head of the Serpent.

And Jesus is our own archetype for being human. In becoming like Him, in following Him, in participating in His life, we become who we were intended to be: bearers of His image, His very own sons and daughters.

REFLECT AND MEDITATE

Consider the power of the Holy Spirit to create life where there was none. And consider how this same Holy Spirit has done this work in you.

Reflect on the humility of God the Son, to be born weak and frail, to pass through blood and water, to hunger and thirst, to need His mother.

Meditate upon the idea that the body is consecrated because Christ has come in the flesh, that humanity is elevated because the King dwelt among us.

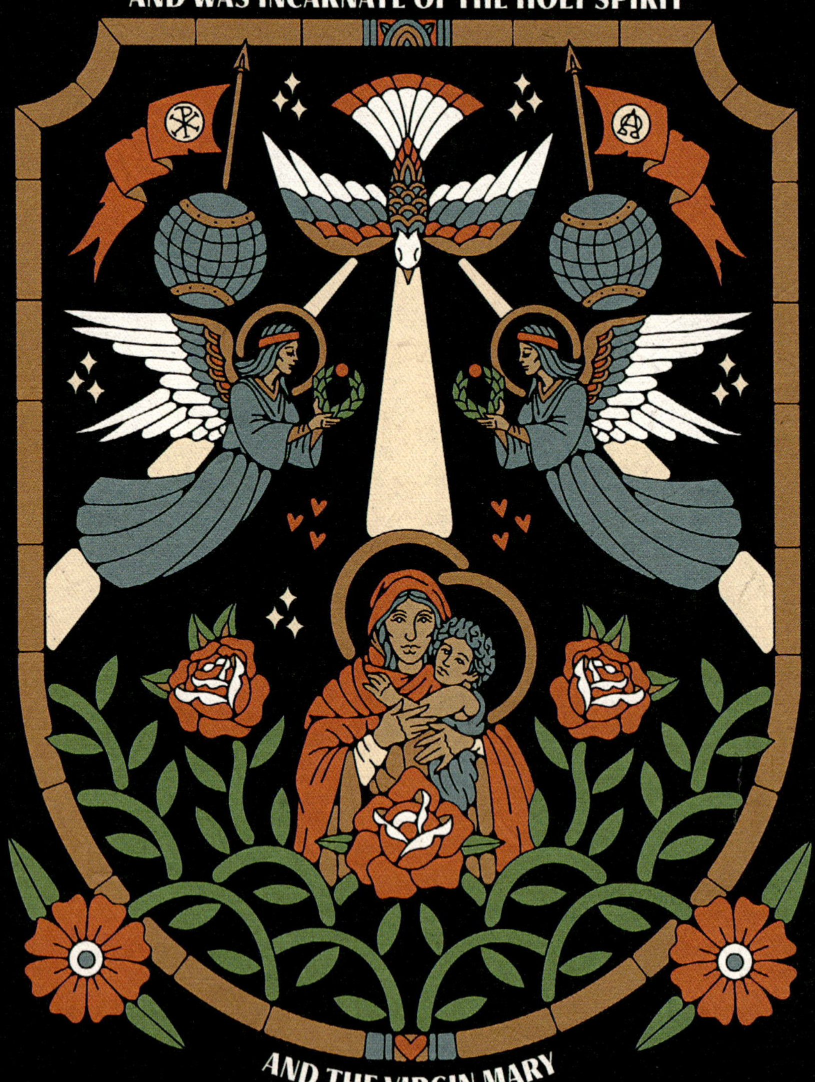
AND WAS INCARNATE OF THE HOLY SPIRIT
AND THE VIRGIN MARY
AND BECAME MAN

DAY 14

This piece features Mary holding her Son, the God-Man, Jesus, as a child. Jesus is a bit older in this depiction than the classic image of swaddling babe. I chose this to reflect the moments He would have longed to be in His Father's house.

Mary and Jesus are shown in a garden that is growing and overwhelming the wilderness. In the wilderness, we hear the voice of John the Baptist calling out, "Make straight the way of the Lord" (John 1:23 KJV). And it is this wilderness that will one day become the New Eden; death and barrenness will burst forth with life and plenty, irrigated by the life of God, a true promised land.

The Holy Spirit shines down in power upon Mary, as it is by the Spirit's power that she became pregnant with the Lord of all the earth—symbolized in the two globes below the dove's wings. Each of the globes has a flag planted upon it. One bears the *alpha* and *omega* emblem, showing that Jesus is the first and the last, the beginning and the end. The other flag bears an early Christian image, the *Chi Rho* (based on the first two letters of *Christ* in Greek), and symbolizes that Jesus is the Messiah.

There are angels beside Mary, and in their hands are victory wreaths with which to crown the King who will triumph over the grave. These angels also call us back to the song Mary sang in response to the news that she would bear Immanuel, God with us, confirmed by her cousin Elizabeth:

> For He has regarded the lowly state of His maidservant; for behold, henceforth all generations will call me blessed. For He who is mighty has done great things for me, and holy is His name. (Luke 1:48–49 NKJV)

REFLECT AND MEDITATE

Consider how Mary gave herself sacrificially, as all mothers do, for her Son. Imagine what it would have meant to be obedient to God, not just in this moment of the incarnation but also in every moment in raising her Son.

Reflect upon what it means for Jesus, the Messiah, to be the first and last, the beginning and the end, and that He will reign over all the earth.

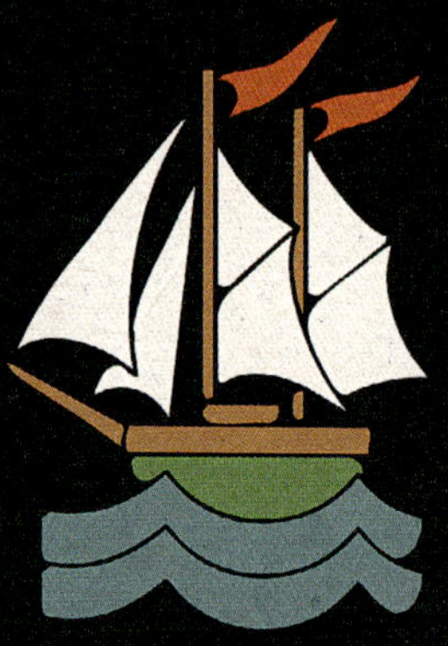

HE WAS CRUCIFIED FOR US UNDER
PONTIUS PILATE . . .

DAY 15

The cross is a curse, as the Scriptures say: "Cursed is everyone who hangs on a tree" (Galatians 3:13 NKJV). For our sake, Jesus took on death; for our sake, and for our salvation, the true King was crucified. This same King who created all things laid down His life at the hands of His creatures.

And the Scriptures maintain that He did this for the *joy* that was set before Him, that He endured this cross, that He scorned its shame—He endured the curse of death so that He might be victorious over it and that we might share in His great victory (Hebrews 12:2).

The Creed appeals to history here, saying that Jesus was executed *under* Pontius Pilate, delivered to him by the chief priests and the elders, the Sanhedrin. It is not some myth, some legend, some old wives' tale; God Himself was to be executed. These chief priests wanted Him dead, killed because He claimed to be King of the Jews, because this Jesus claimed to be the Promised Messiah.

And so the God-Man, Jesus, walked the *Via Dolorosa*, the Sorrowful Way, up to the Place of the Skull, Golgotha, and was lifted up on the cross, between earth and heaven. In that space where heaven and earth overlap (and they overlap fully in Him), darkness fell, and Jesus breathed His last: "Into Your hands I commit My spirit" (Luke 23:46 NKJV).

This lifting up echoes Moses lifting the bronze serpent, that all who look to Jesus will have eternal life (Numbers 21:4–9). And this cross is also the fulfillment of Jacob's Ladder (Genesis 28:10–22)—the very way to connect earth and heaven, the very way to reconcile humanity back to our Father.

The veil is torn. It is finished. This cross bore the *true* God, and the nails through His hands and feet pierced the divine, and yet the cross could not destroy God. Athanasius said this:

> And He was witnessed to as Master of Creation, in that the Sun withdrew his beams and the earth trembled and the rocks were rent, and the executioners recognized that the Crucified was truly Son of God. For the Body they beheld was not that of some man, but of God, being in which, even when being crucified, He raised the dead.[1]

Jesus, the God-Man, suffered death—His soul separated from His body—for our sake and for our salvation. As Hebrews 2:9 says, "But we see Jesus, who was made a little lower than the angels, for the suffering of death crowned with glory and honor, that He, by the grace of God, might taste death for everyone" (NKJV).

REFLECT AND MEDITATE

Reflect upon the Creator becoming accursed by hanging on the tree. And consider that the author of life gave up His life at the hands of His creation.

Meditate on the Sorrowful Way, the path our Lord took up to the mountain of death. Imagine His thoughts about the world, about His people, about even you.

Ponder what it means for Jesus and the cross to be a new kind of Jacob's Ladder, a new center bridging heaven and earth.

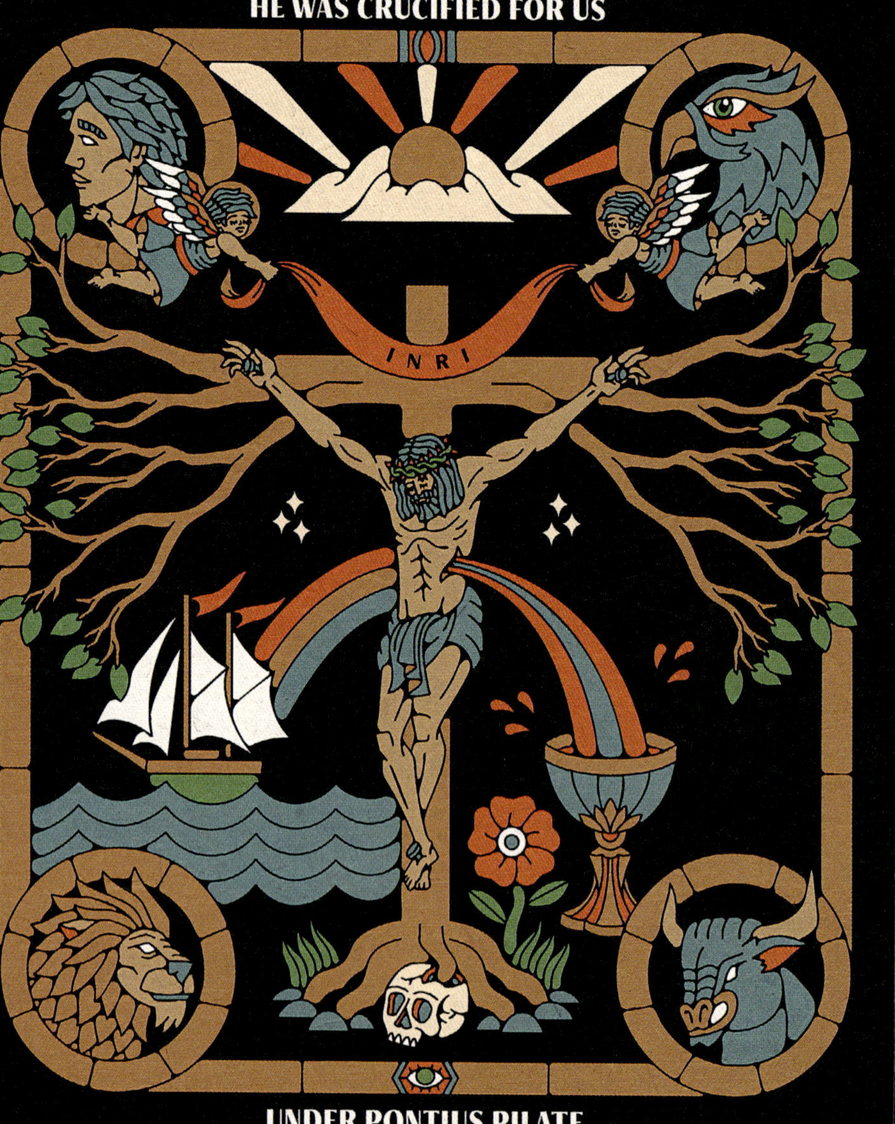
HE WAS CRUCIFIED FOR US
INRI
UNDER PONTIUS PILATE

DAY 16

This piece features the Lord Jesus crucified upon the cross, a crown of thorns placed upon His head, hands and feet pieced, side bleeding from His wounds. Above Him, normally hammered to the stipes, is a banner held up by angels, and it reads, *INRI*: *Jesus the Nazarene, King of the Jews* (or in Latin, *Iesus Nazarenus Rex Iudaeorum*).

This cross is a tree, considered to be a curse, but Jesus redeems it and transforms this instrument of death, revealing it to be the true Tree of Life. And if we feast from the fruits of this Tree, we shall never die.

The cross has roots that stretch down into the earth, where the skull of Adam remains. Adam, and those who are in him, remain under the enslavement of death, under the tyranny of the grave. But these roots are growing through this skull, and Jesus, the Second Adam, is making all things new. And from this earth, this grave, emerges a flower, a sign that new life is coming.

Framing the canvas are the four symbols of the Gospels: Matthew as a winged man, Mark as a winged lion, Luke as an ox, and John as an eagle. These gospel accounts tell the story of Jesus, of His life and death and His crucifixion, that for our sake and for our salvation, Jesus laid down His life. They retell the good news, proclaiming that He faced death *for us*, instead of us facing death, because we could never defeat that great Enemy.

From His wounded sides flow blood and water. The water pours out as a flood, in which an ark, the true ark, rides over the torrent to bring peace and order and salvation, echoing the words of Peter (1 Peter 3:20–22).

And the blood empties into a chalice, a symbol of the Last Supper, in which Jesus said, "This cup is the new covenant in My blood, which is shed for you" (Luke 22:20 NKJV). This raised cup is a welcoming, an acclamation, a toast to the victory of our Christ.

REFLECT AND MEDITATE

Reflect upon how Christ transforms the cursed tree, scorning its shame, and makes it a new and better Tree of Life.

Consider the juxtaposition of Adam, who rejected the Tree of Life and is now dead, and Christ, the Second Adam, who is the fruit of the new Tree of Life, who gives Himself up for us that we might find His life.

Reflect on what it means to participate in the life and death of Jesus in the two great sacraments of the church: the holy supper and baptism.

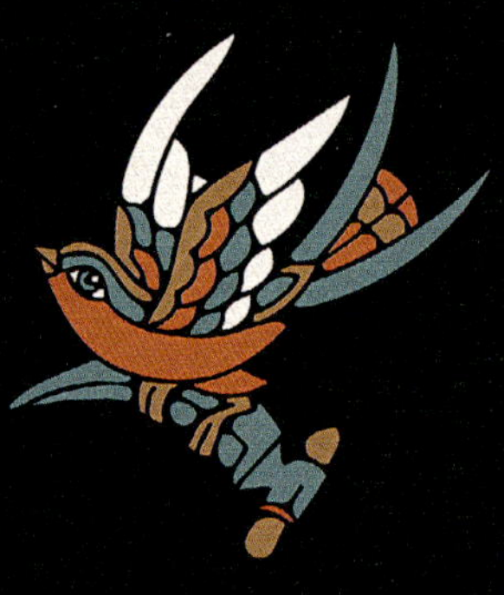

. . . HE SUFFERED AND WAS BURIED . . .

DAY 17

Jesus died.

This death was a separation, proof of the true humanity of Jesus. His body was taken down from the cross, wrapped in clean linens, and laid in the tomb of Joseph of Arimathea. And darkness fell. Even the sun and lights of heaven bowed their heads.

Death is no easy undertaking. To willingly face the grave is a true work of courage and bravery. To face suffering, to confront death itself, requires valor of the highest kind.

Christ suffered *bravely.*

He bled and died courageously.

He stared down death as a man. With no whimper, but with face set like flint, His heel crushed the Serpent's head. I have seen courage in the eyes of men—I have seen the fire—and maybe death and the grave saw those same burning eyes when our Christ descended, seeking victory.

The Creed says that He was buried, and during this time of silence between the crucifixion and the resurrection, Jesus descended into the realm of the dead, into Hades.

There is an icon that depicts this, the icon of the Resurrection, or the *Harrowing of Hades. Harrowing* is an old word for "making desolate." The Lord Jesus descended into Hades, as the apostles say, and He liberated the souls of the just from their captivity.

He tread down the gates of hell.

He shattered the ancient locks.

He led His people up out of death's domain.

He was victorious.

REFLECT AND MEDITATE

Reflect upon the bravery of Christ. Imagine His smile as He was out on the Sea of Galilee with His friends, and imagine His eyes when He walked up the steep mount of Golgotha for us and for our salvation.

Imagine the joy set before Him, to descend to the grave and to shatter the ancient gates that held His people captive. Imagine Him grabbing Adam and Eve and all the rest by the wrists and leading them home to paradise.

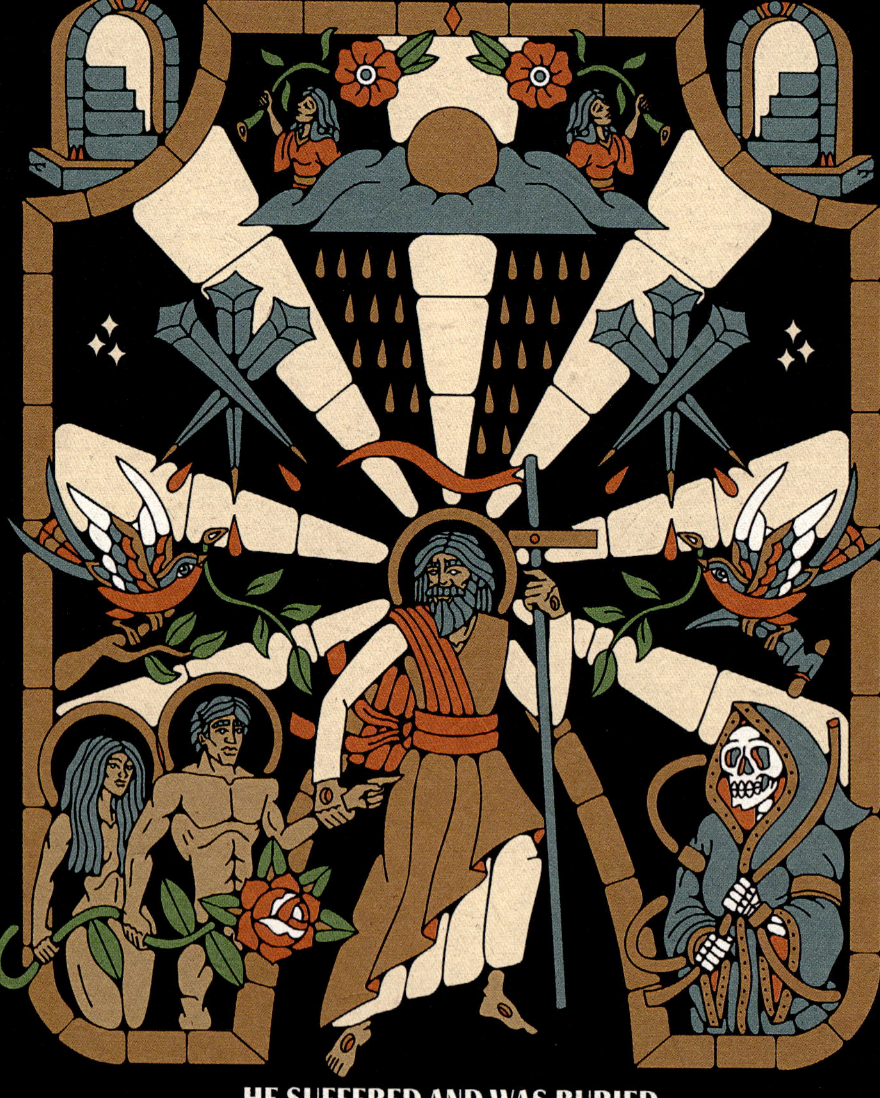

HE SUFFERED AND WAS BURIED

DAY 18

This piece is my own rendering of the *Harrowing of Hades.*

In it we see Christ, nail-pierced hands and feet, emerging from a mandorla, an almond-shaped frame signifying God's bright glory and majesty, and this glory bursts forth in light all around the image. This is the victorious Christ—the Hero of humanity.

Jesus is lifting Adam and Eve, who represent all of humanity, out of the grave, and they are holding a flower, symbolizing the new and coming Eden. Death is shackled on the other side of Christ, bound by chains, and his sickle is shattered: "O Death, where is your sting? O Hades, where is your victory?" (1 Corinthians 15:55 NKJV).

Above Jesus, on either side, are singing doves, echoes of the birds sent out of the ark in the time of Noah. Each one is holding bits of branch and leaves, denoting that there is an end to the storm. There is a coming promised land. There will be rest.

Further up are nails, the nails used to crucify the Son of God, and they now drip blood—a symbol that this blood gives life, that this blood, God's own blood, was shed for us, and by His stripes we, and the whole cosmos, are healed.

At the top of the image are the heavens; a new day is rising, and the life of heaven is raining down. On either side of the frame are gateways that we freely choose to take—either the path into life or the path into death.

REFLECT AND MEDITATE

Reflect on Adam and Eve being lifted by the wrists—not by their strength but by grace. Consider what it means that you, too, were grasped and raised by the hand of Christ.

Contemplate the broken sickle of death, the shattered gates of Hades. Let yourself feel the immensity of Christ's courage as He descended to the grave not as a prisoner but as a conqueror.

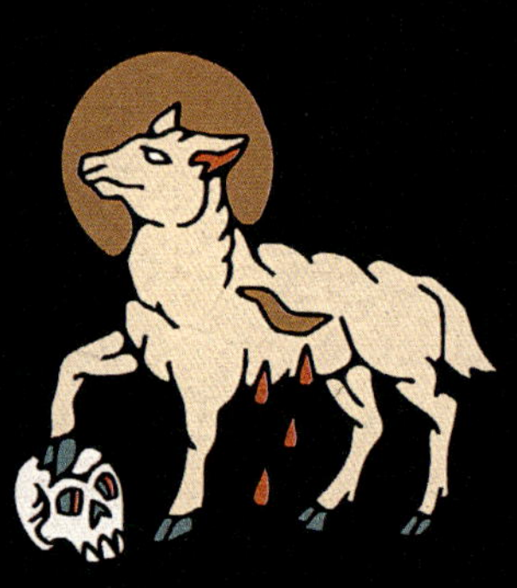

HE ROSE ON THE THIRD DAY,
ACCORDING TO THE SCRIPTURES.

DAY 19

The grave could not hold the Son of God. Death's sickle was shattered, its robes torn apart and shredded. Christ has risen. This is the heart of the Christian faith: the resurrection of our Lord and King. Jesus is the "firstfruits" of the resurrection (1 Corinthians 15:20 NKJV), and for all who are in Him, we will follow His path. That which is corruptible will put on incorruption. Mortality will be swallowed up by immortality. We will be raised with Him into newness of life, for Christ is the King of the living.

Jesus said that He would lay down His life freely and that just as He had the authority to lay down His life, so, too, He had the power to take it up again (John 10:18). He has authority over death. And He, forever, remains our Mediator because of His indestructible life (Hebrews 7:16).

The women went to the tomb, tears in their eyes, carrying spices to honor the body of their Lord. But when they arrived, the stone was rolled away and His body was gone.

Two men in shining garments appeared beside them, saying,

> Why do you seek the living among the dead? He is not here, but is risen! Remember how He spoke to you when He was still

> in Galilee, saying, "The Son of Man must be delivered into the hands of sinful men, and be crucified, and the third day rise again." (Luke 24:5–7 NKJV)

And the women went away and ran home, rejoicing and singing the new song of the resurrection.

All of this—the crucifying, the suffering, the burial, the rising again—was done "in accordance with the Scriptures" (1 Corinthians 15:3–4 ESV). This was God's plan of redemption, woven from the beginning: the plan to reconcile heaven and earth.

But the Creed does more than tell us it was God's plan. The Creed tells us that resurrection is real. The Gospels are rooted in history. The life, death, and resurrection of Jesus are not just spiritual ideas. Redemption unfolded in real places, through real people, in real time. You can hear the echoes in history and catch the confessions of the witnesses, still carried on the wind.

This is what Lewis and Tolkien meant when they said "myth became fact."[1]

The greatest story, written deep on every human heart, is the story of the Hero who faces the dragon, the King who rescues His people, the God who dies and rises. Hope breaking into history. The myth that became flesh and blood. And Christ is our true hero, killing the ancient Serpent, rescuing His people, giving life and light.

REFLECT AND MEDITATE

Reflect upon this new time: a time of victory. We tend to imagine all of history from this side of the resurrection, but there was a time before it. A time before death was conquered, before the gates of heaven were opened. A time when the stone still sealed the tomb.

Take a moment to rest in this moment of victory, to stand at the empty tomb, like the women did, in wonder and awe.

HE ROSE ON THE THIRD DAY,

IC XC NIKA

ACCORDING TO THE SCRIPTURES.

DAY 20

The risen Christ emerges as the focal point of this piece. His royal scepter has a banner, and written upon it: *IC XC NIKA*, or "Jesus Christ Conquers." Death and grave are defeated, symbolized as skulls on either side of Him, completely overwhelmed by new life.

The wounds of Christ now glow bright gold. Wounds that were a shame, scars that would be a disgrace to any other king, are now the shining emblems of victory. And Jesus is holding up His hand of blessing; His life is the true blessing that we now get to partake in.

At the bottom of this image are a lion and a slain lamb, a depiction of Revelation 5:5–6, which describes the strength of the Lion of the tribe of Judah and how the Root of David has triumphed. And when John the Revelator looked, he saw a lamb, as if it had been slain. This is our Christ, the sacrificial lamb and the conquering lion.

Above in the heavens, on either side of the Holy Spirit, are the living creatures crying out: "Worthy is the Lamb who was slain to receive power and riches and wisdom, and strength and honor and glory and blessing!" (Revelation 5:12 NKJV).

All of heaven is roaring in victorious celebration, many thousands upon thousands, then thousands times ten thousands—and then the whole created order shouts out: "To him who sits on the throne and to the Lamb be praise and honor and glory and power, for ever and ever!" (v. 13 NIV).

REFLECT AND MEDITATE

Reflect upon the wounds of Christ that are now His glory, the wounds in which the apostle Thomas placed his hands and then proclaimed Jesus to be the true Christ (John 20:24–29). And consider what it means that Jesus transforms death into life, even in your own life, and how your scars might be badges of honor in the life to come.

Imagine for a moment the sound of heaven. The ecstatic cheering—the King is victorious. Take a moment to join in their song.

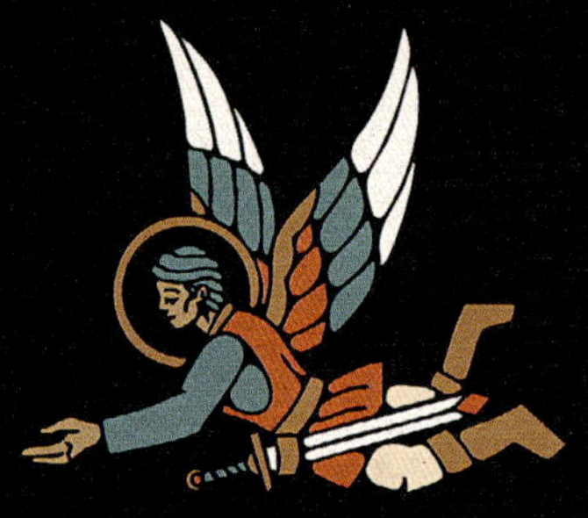

HE ASCENDED INTO HEAVEN
AND IS SEATED AT THE RIGHT HAND
OF THE FATHER.

DAY 21

This is the continuation of the resurrection—up from the grave and ascending, returning to the Father's side in victory, His mission accomplished. Christ descended, *came down* from heaven, and made His dwelling, or tabernacled, with us. Then He descended further still, obedient to death, even death on a cross, and entered the realm of the dead. And as He rose from the dead, so, too, does He ascend back up into the heavens in glory.

It is finished.

Acts 1:3 tells us that Jesus remained on earth for forty days, speaking to His listeners about the kingdom of God. He ate and drank with His friends, and He told them of all truth. After this time, He was taken up in a great cloud to the heavens. And two men in white robes called out to all those watching, "Men of Galilee, why do you stand gazing up into heaven? This same Jesus, who was taken up from you into heaven, will so come in like manner as you saw Him go into heaven" (Acts 1:11 NKJV).

Christ sits now in ruling authority at His Father's side, at His right hand, forever the God-Man with dominion over all the cosmos. This right hand not only carries authority; it carries with it blessing, just as Jacob laid his right hand on Ephraim's head in blessing (Genesis 48:14–20). You can almost hear the Father repeat, "This is My beloved Son, with whom I am well pleased; listen to Him!" (Matthew 17:5 NASB). Christ's throne is above every throne, the King of all kings:

> Therefore God exalted him to the highest place and gave him the name that is above every name, that at the name of Jesus every knee should bow, in heaven and on earth and under the earth, and every tongue acknowledge that Jesus Christ is Lord, to the glory of God the Father. (Philippians 2:9–11 NIV)

And this reign, this kingdom, will have no end. Now you and I live in this reality, Christ enthroned above all powers and dominions and authorities. We live in bright hope of a victorious Christ. He will lead us home.

> The Son is the radiance of God's glory and the exact representation of his being, sustaining all things by his powerful word. After he had provided purification for sins, he sat down at the right hand of the Majesty in heaven. (Hebrews 1:3 NIV)

REFLECT AND MEDITATE

Reflect upon the mission of Christ: coming down from heaven into a womb, being made flesh, living and dying and descending to Hades. And consider Him taking up His own life and then being caught up in the clouds to return to His place of authority for our sake and for our salvation.

Imagine supping with the risen Christ, fish cooking over an open fire on the shores of the sea. Imagine all that He would say to you.

Consider what it means to live in the kingdom of Christ, a kingdom inaugurated but not yet consummated. Meditate upon how you might join the work of tearing down strongholds in the name of your King.

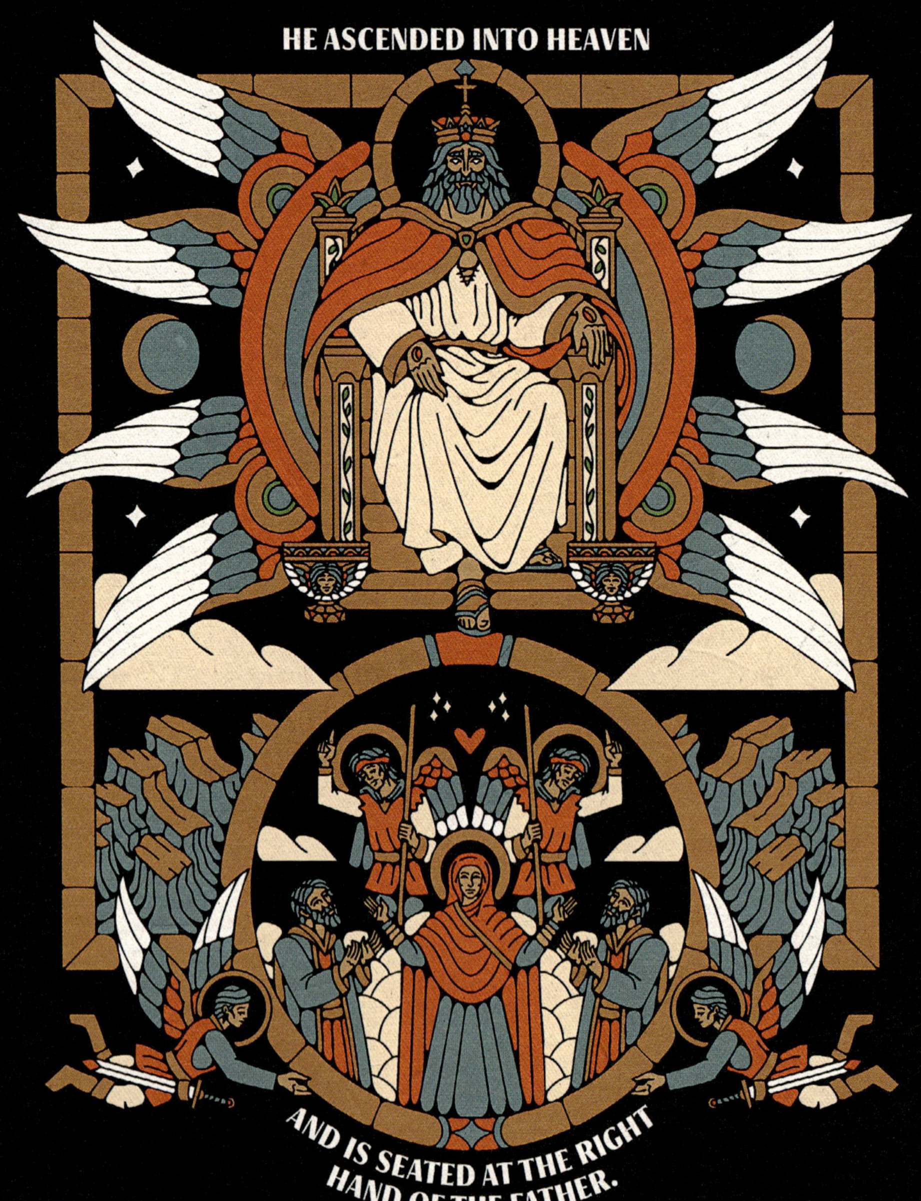
HE ASCENDED INTO HEAVEN
AND IS SEATED AT THE RIGHT
HAND OF THE FATHER.

DAY 22

In this image, we see Peter and Paul looking up, watching their Lord ascend. This is symbolic—Paul was not present at the Ascension. These two, with Mary in between them, represent the entirety of the Church—"first to the Jew, then to the Gentile" (Romans 1:16 NIV)—all made one. The angels are announcing that Jesus will one day return, just as He came.

Framing this scene is a desert wilderness with some angels, reminiscent of the annunciation of the incarnation. This is a parallel to that scene, but in reverse, where the King returns to His rightful place as Lord of all.

Above are the clouds, the ones that carried Jesus to the side of His Father, denoting that this throne is above all thrones, above the heavens.

Christ is seated in glory upon the throne, robed and victorious. His throne is surrounded by rainbows, referencing Ezekiel 1:28 and Revelation 4:3—the rainbow brilliant and shining like an emerald.

In Scripture, rainbows are more than color—more than *beauty*—they are symbols of a covenant. Here, the rainbow recalls the promise in Genesis 9:13–16, when God set His bow in the clouds;

the war-bow of judgment is now hung in peace, faced away from the earth. Here the rainbow crowned around Christ signifies the fullness of that peace, the complete and final covenant of love.

Surrounding the throne are the wings of the four living creatures who worship the Lord, the same four beings mentioned in Revelation 4:6–8. The stars in the sky symbolize the heavenly host joining in the song.

REFLECT AND MEDITATE

Meditate upon the bright glory of the victorious Christ, the One who shines like jasper and ruby, the one whose throne is encircled in a bright rainbow shining like an emerald.

And consider the fullness of the promises of God, the covenant with Noah: to be fruitful and multiply, to be at peace, and to subdue the earth and make it Eden. Think of how this covenant finds its fulfillment in the new covenant of Christ.

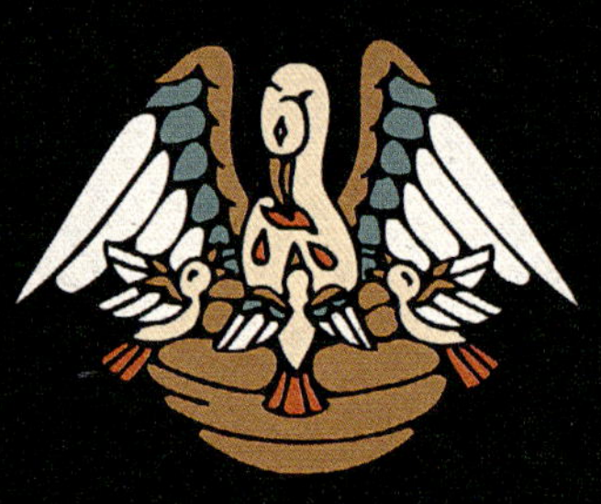

HE WILL COME AGAIN WITH GLORY
TO JUDGE THE LIVING AND THE DEAD

DAY 23

Ours is the time in between, the time of waiting and remaining. The already and the not yet. The kingdom has been established, the Church has been instituted, but it has not yet been spread throughout all the earth. It has not yet been consummated. For this in-between time, we wait for Him in faith, following His way, believing in His words, and showing our loyalty through love.

But the time will come when our Lord returns, and it will not be like His first coming. It will not be in humility.

He will come again in glory on a white horse, clad and strong, His name called Faithful and True. His eyes blazing like fire, set against His foes, making war until every last enemy is put beneath His feet and He is crowned as King. He is the Word of God. His robe, dipped in blood, flutters like a banner behind Him as He rides His white mare. And all the armies of heaven follow after Him. The end of all things is near. Emblazoned on His robe and on His thigh is "KING OF KINGS AND LORD OF LORDS" (Revelation 19:16 NKJV). The trumpets sound, and the armies of heaven roar. Victory dawns, as Revelation 19 tells us.

When Christ returns, He will come to make an end to His

enemies, to destroy sin and death and Satan. He will come to lead His people into the fullness of His kingdom of light.

And all will rise and be judged by the Lord.

In Daniel 7:9–10, the prophet saw a vision: The throne of God is authoritative over all thrones. The Ancient of Days, God the Father, burned forth with flaming majesty. The court was seated, and the books were opened. And here the Creed says that Christ Himself, the Son of Man, will take up this role at the end of ages. He will execute the judgments of the Father. As Revelation 20:13 declares: "The sea gave up the dead which were in it; and death and hell delivered up the dead which were in them: and they were judged every man according to their works" (KJV).

Those who followed Christ, who joined with Him by faith working itself out in love (Galatians 5:6), will be welcomed. And those who rejected Christ, who scorned His way and spurned His gift of life, will experience God as a consuming fire, and they will be cut off from the Tree of Life forever.

REFLECT AND MEDITATE

Meditate upon the glorious return of Christ, with the armies of heaven set out to destroy injustice and sin and death and all works of Satan. This will be the final march of heaven's armies, the last battle—and in the end, we triumph.

Ponder your own life and your own faith, expressed in loyal love. The apostle Paul warns us that we work out our salvation in fear and trembling (Philippians 2:12), while also taking full hope in the grace and mercy of God. Feel the weight of this tension: a trembling awe before the judgment seat of Christ and a child's confidence before the Father of lights. Then commit anew to the path of light: the narrow way that leads to life.

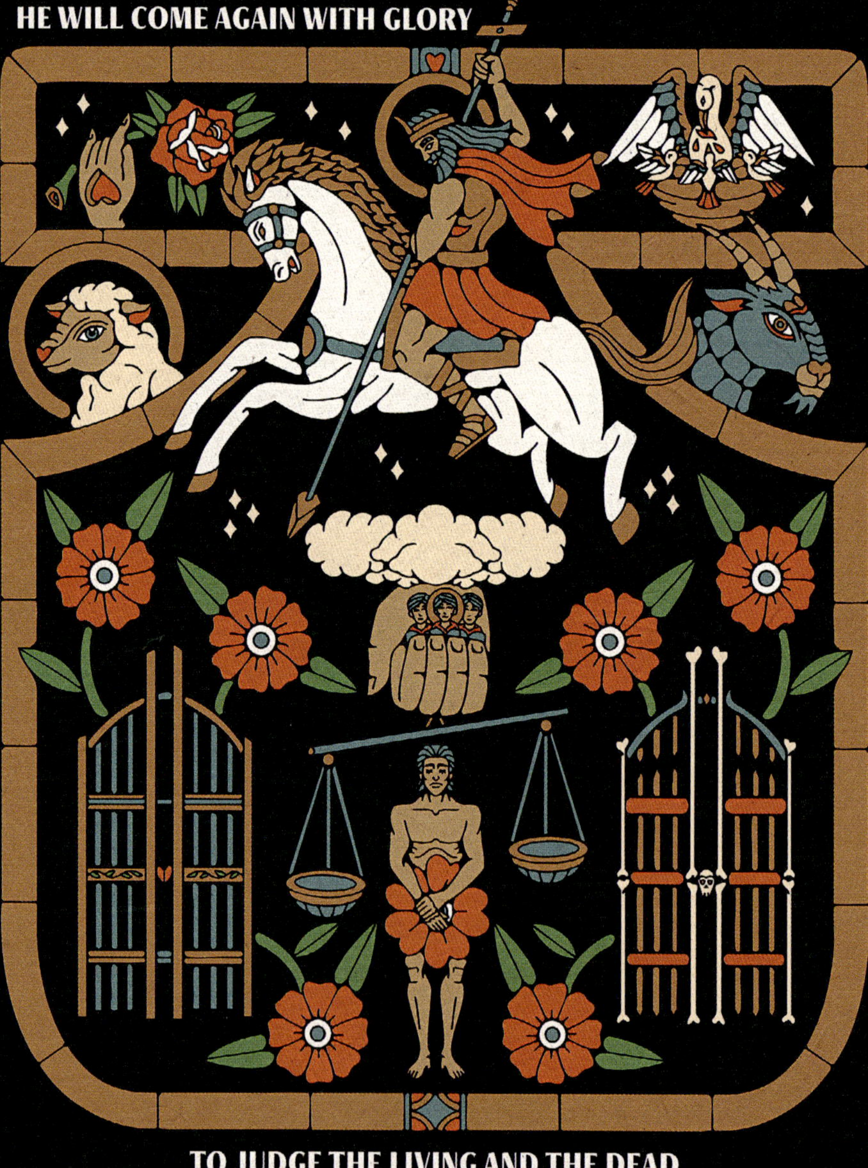
HE WILL COME AGAIN WITH GLORY
TO JUDGE THE LIVING AND THE DEAD

DAY 24

In this image, we see Christ riding on a white horse, eyes shining as fire, and a spear in His hands to strike down His enemies. On either side of the Lord, at the top, are symbolic representations of His worthiness to execute judgment. Worthy is the slain lamb, pictured in the pelican that lays itself down to feed its chicks, and the wounds of Love that feed us and lead us to life.

And also on the left and right of Christ are images of a sheep and a goat, depicting what Jesus said in Matthew 25: "All the nations will be gathered before Him, and He will separate them one from another, as a shepherd divides his sheep from the goats. And He will set the sheep on His right hand, but the goats on the left" (vv. 32–33 NKJV).

Christ is riding on the clouds of glory, and below Him coming down from the clouds is the hand of God holding the scales of judgment. In the Byzantine-style icons that depict this, the demons are trying to tip the scales toward death, but God will judge both fairly and truly, according to what Christ continues to say in Matthew 25:

> Then the King will say to those on His right hand, "Come, you blessed of My Father, inherit the kingdom prepared for you

> from the foundation of the world: for I was hungry and you gave Me food; I was thirsty and you gave Me drink; I was a stranger and you took Me in; I was naked and you clothed Me; I was sick and you visited Me; I was in prison and you came to Me." (vv. 34–36 NKJV)

The man depicted in the image is every human who will face the judgment, who will stand before the throne, some with Christ and in Christ and some not.

On either side of the man are gates; on the left are the ancient gates of paradise—stones, inspired by Psalm 24, that are shining and bursting forth with life. On the right are the gates that lead to death, with skulls and bones depicting bondage and punishment.

REFLECT AND MEDITATE

Reflect upon that great day. The Day of Judgment isn't normally a devotional topic, but it is important for us to feel the weight of it. Imagine yourself there, and consider everything you might feel.

Reflect upon your own life and all the ways you might give cups of cold water in Jesus' name, ways you might express your faith in love and make Jesus known.

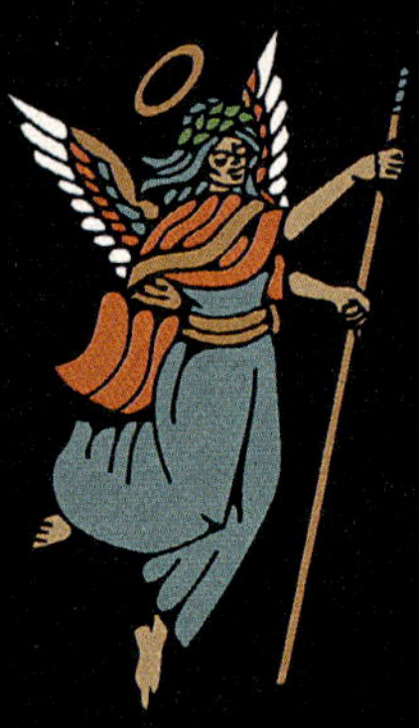

HIS KINGDOM SHALL HAVE NO END.

DAY 25

In his Gospel, Mark quoted Jesus saying: "And then shall they see the Son of man coming in the clouds with great power and glory" (13:26 KJV). This is an allusion to Daniel 7:13–14, and the full quote is worth considering:

> And there before me was one like a son of man, coming with the clouds of heaven. He approached the Ancient of Days and was led into his presence. He was given authority, glory and sovereign power; all nations and peoples of every language worshiped him. His dominion is an everlasting dominion that will not pass away, and his kingdom is one that will never be destroyed. (NIV)

This scripture is fulfilled in the life, death, burial, resurrection, and ascension of the Lord Jesus Christ, the Son of Man, who was given all authority. This kingdom is forever, unlike the kings of old who died, betrayed their people, or were defeated by their enemies. And these kingdoms around us today—no matter how strong they seem—will crumble and fall. The promise made to David in 2 Samuel 7:11–16, that a son of his will sit on the throne forever, was fulfilled in Christ, the true Son of David. Jesus is the King because

He has conquered every enemy, because His life cannot be taken, for He is life itself.

This kingdom will be for all people, all nations of every language and every time. The mission of Christ is for *all* humanity, and His kingdom welcomes *everyone* home. And He will reign over His beloved people.

This is not a tyranny; it is neither subjugation nor oppression. This kingdom is not made up of curfews, slavery, or authoritarian control. This kingdom is a reflection of the character of God as displayed by Christ during His time here on earth:

Love.
Holiness.
Grace.
Kindness.

These will mark His eternal kingdom. It will be saturated in His goodness, replete with His beauty, and rooted in His truth. And we will all thrive under the power of our great King.

This is the fulfillment of the Lord's Prayer, as well: "Your kingdom come" (Matthew 6:10 NKJV). The kingdom of heaven will come down to earth, and that which was once divided will be unified again by Christ. A full overlap of heaven and earth—God with us, forever, in all places at all times. Eden restored and magnified infinitely.

REFLECT AND MEDITATE

Imagine the Son of Man appearing before the Ancient of Days and receiving full authority, glory, and sovereignty. Imagine the worship of a people, long oppressed by sin and death. Imagine their joy and jubilation at the true King who will reign in love and kindness. And imagine the peace of knowing that this kingdom will not end, that there will be everlasting harmony.

Reflect upon the full overlap of heaven and earth and how everything is a sign that points to this great truth. God dwelt with man in the garden, Soon we will not see or participate in part. We will enjoy full communion with our King.

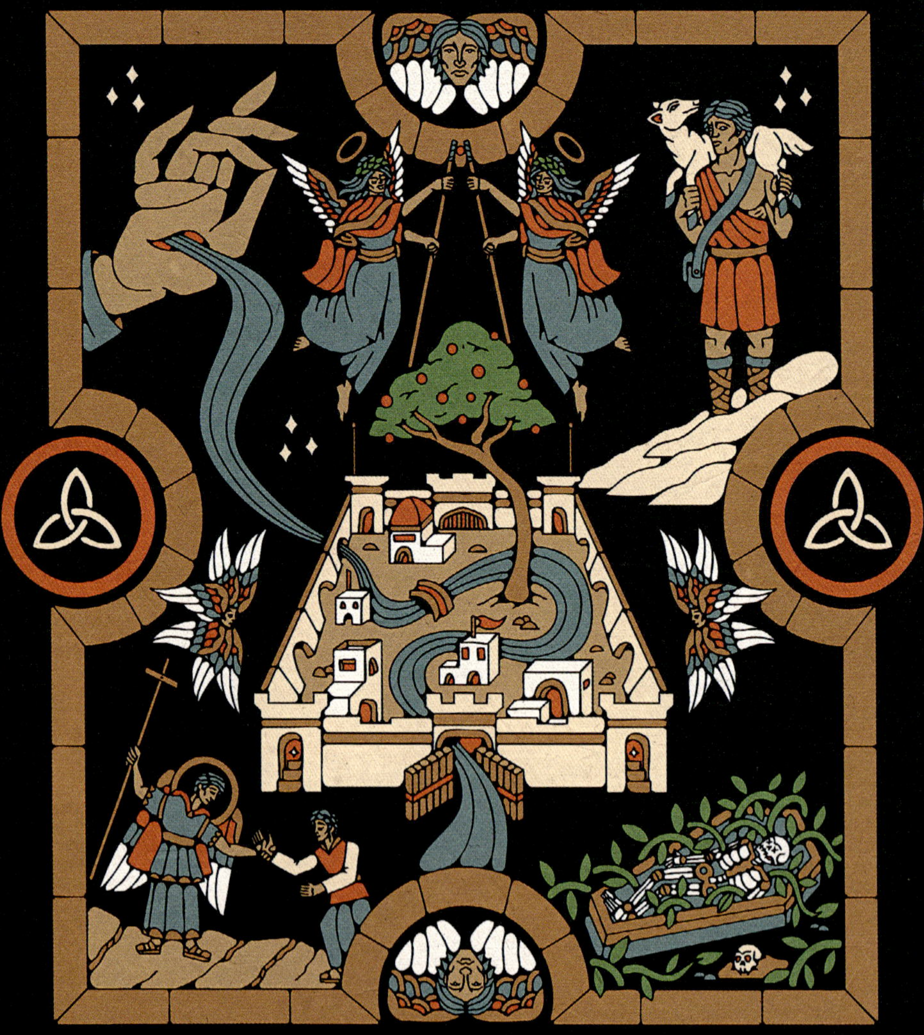
HIS KINGDOM
SHALL HAVE NO END.

DAY 26

In this piece, we see the New and coming Jerusalem, the city of peace, laid out as a square or a cube. The only other cube featured in the Bible is the holy of holies, a place in the tabernacle that only priests could enter—and only once a year, lest they be consumed. But this new city, the city for all the redeemed, is the new holy of holies. And we all can enter freely because of Christ, to enjoy the presence of God eternally.

This city is for all the redeemed, as displayed in the twelve gates, symbolizing the twelve tribes and the twelve apostles. In the center of this city is a tree that feeds the people of God. And a river runs through it, which is supposed to come from the throne of God (Revelation 22:1)—yet in this piece, it comes from the wounds of Christ, to represent the slain Lamb who is worthy of reigning on the throne.

The top right of the image features the Good Shepherd, the one who finds His lost sheep and brings them into the fold. Angels above and beside the city are still acting as ministering spirits of God for humanity.

At the bottom of the image, on the left, we see the angel guiding

John the Revelator, showing him this heavenly vision. Most of the life to come is described to us by *negations*—there will be no more death, no more mourning, no more crying, no more pain (Revelation 21:4). It is by what will be absent that we glimpse the peace and purity of the kingdom. And so, part of what John saw remains a mystery, one that is hopeful and filled with light.

On the right side of the image is a skeleton in a coffin, overgrown and decaying. There will be no more death, for the old order of things has gone away. The new order of the kingdom of Christ is one of life and light.

Embedded in the frame of this image are symbols of the Trinity and winged angels, denoting the freedom to love completely. This city is governed by the triune God, filled with a love that sets us free.

REFLECT AND MEDITATE

Reflect upon what a gift it is to dwell freely in the presence of God forever.

Consider what it will be like to enjoy the fullness of God with all of the redeemed throughout all of history. Imagine meeting your heroes of the faith. Imagine all of humanity as the new and true family of God.

Think of how this kingdom will never end and how all your striving will be turned to rest.

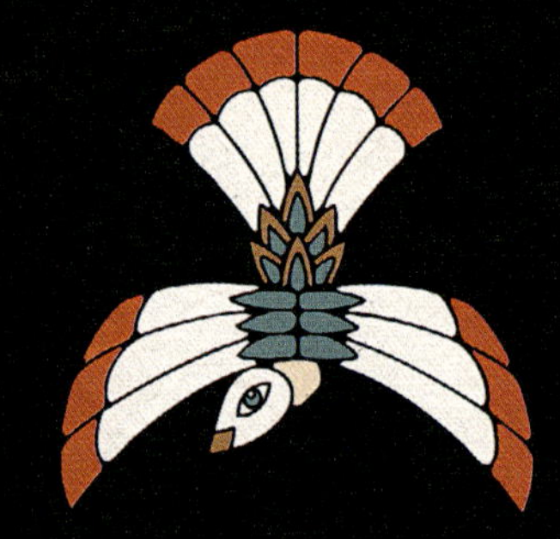

WE BELIEVE IN THE HOLY SPIRIT,
THE LORD,
THE CREATOR OF LIFE . . .

DAY 27

The Creed moves now to the final person of the Trinity, the Holy Spirit. This Holy Spirit, whom we believe in together as the Church, is the Spirit of the Lord.

In the Old Testament we saw the Spirit hovering over the waters at creation. We saw Him rushing upon men like a mighty wind, empowering them for great works: the building of the tabernacle and the great victories of Samson, Gideon, and Joshua.

But under the old covenant, the Spirit's working was not permanent, not that kind of internal transformation. David prayed, "Do not take Your Holy Spirit from me" (Psalm 51:11 NKJV).

And yet the prophets of old spoke of a coming day, a coming promise, that the Spirit would be poured out and bring life, that the very breath of God would regenerate dry bones into living beings. In Jeremiah 31:33, God promised that His law would no longer be written only on stone tablets but upon human hearts, a covenant better than the one received at Sinai.

This is the promise from Ezekiel 36:

> I will give you a new heart, and a new spirit I will put within you. And I will remove the heart of stone from your flesh and

> give you a heart of flesh. And I will put my Spirit within you, and cause you to walk in my statutes and be careful to obey my rules. (vv. 26–27 ESV)

These promises of new life in the old covenant come to fulfilment in the gift of the Holy Spirit. Just as humanity was first filled with the breath of God in Genesis, so, too, is the new humanity—the new covenant community—filled with life from on high. Our bodies are now temples, the place where God Himself dwells.

When Jesus ascended, He promised that the Spirit would come, our Helper and Comforter. And Jesus promised that the Spirit would teach us all things and bring to our remembrance every word He had spoken. The Holy Spirit is present with us, He helps us, and He intercedes for all the saints:

> Likewise the Spirit also helps in our weaknesses. For we do not know what we should pray for as we ought, but the Spirit Himself makes intercession for us with groanings which cannot be uttered. (Romans 8:26 NKJV)

The same Spirit who raised Christ from the grave now raises us into newness of life—and He fills us with the same strength and power, contending with us over death and sin.

REFLECT AND MEDITATE

Consider that the Holy Spirit is always with you, strengthening, reminding, teaching, and leading you in the way that leads to life.

Reflect upon the Spirit's work in redemptive history. Consider the blessing it is to receive God into yourself, to be a moving tabernacle, a place where the presence of God resides.

Meditate upon the very prayers the Holy Spirit utters for you, to express that which is inexpressible, even the things you do not know about yourself.

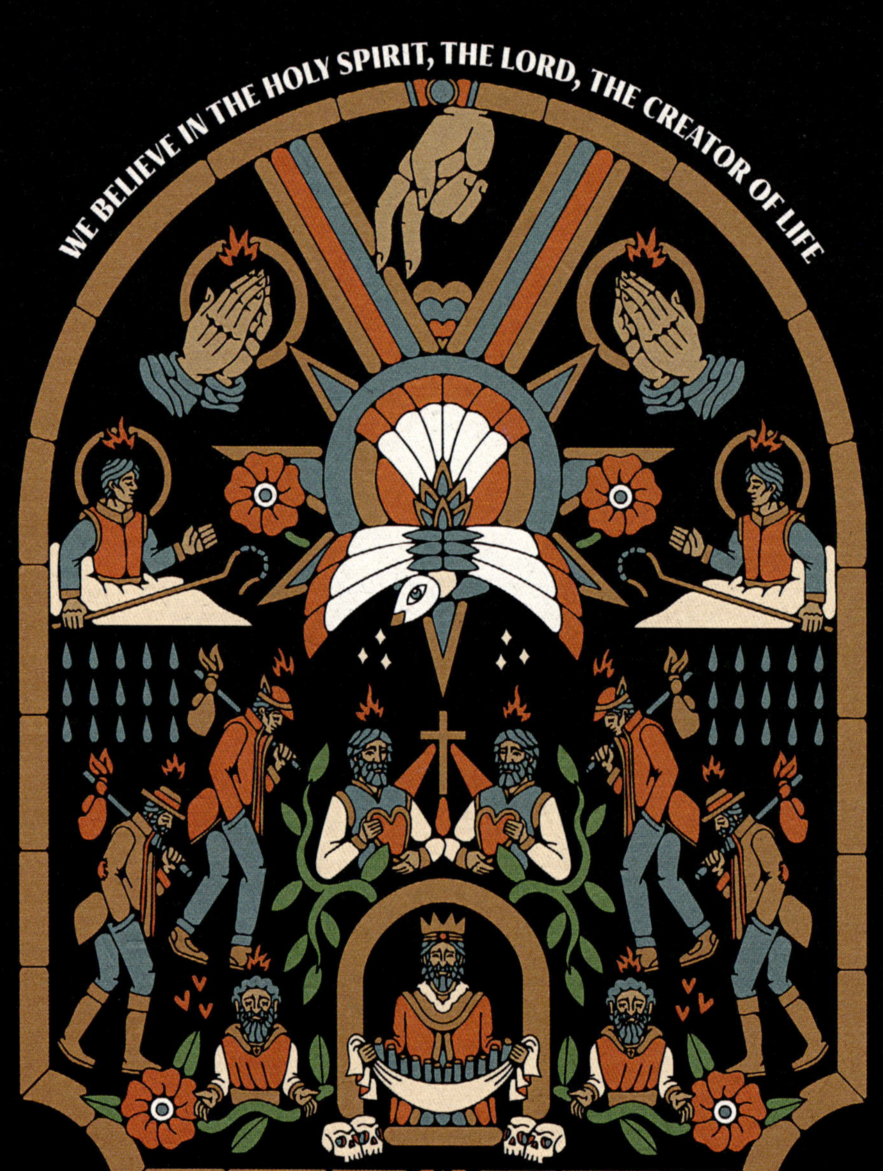
WE BELIEVE IN THE HOLY SPIRIT, THE LORD, THE CREATOR OF LIFE

DAY 28

The Holy Spirit, like a mighty, rushing wind, descended on the day of Pentecost as described in Acts 2. In this piece, the Holy Spirit—represented as a dove, as in the baptism of Christ—shines with the same glorious light as the Father and the Son. His wings are outstretched, overshadowing humanity.

At the top is the hand of the Father, blessing the Spirit, in reference to John 14:26: "But the Helper, the Holy Spirit, whom the Father will send in My name, He will teach you all things, and bring to your remembrance all things that I said to you" (NKJV).

There are thirteen figures in this piece. Twelve of them have the symbolic tongues of fire above their heads, referencing the upper room and the apostles empowered for kingdom mission. Above, there are hands praying in the Spirit and communing with God. Then there are shepherds symbolized, empowered by the Spirit to tend to the flock. Then we see a set of four pilgrims, or sojourners, made strong to endure the upward call of God in Christ by the strength of the Spirit. At the center are two men, full of love, the same love displayed at the cross, a true gift given by the Spirit for our fellow man, to see the world as God does. And lastly, at the bottom, we see two men praying in love, connected to the vine, showing that we remain in Christ by the might of the Spirit.

The final aspect of this piece features a man in a cave, my rendition of part of the icon of Pentecost. Icons are not just art; they are windows into truth, theology painted into matter. They are an invitation into prayer and contemplation.

This icon was originally painted to depict a world without faith. The man in the dark place is crushed under the weight of age and sin, and this is my rendition of that man. The icon describes the symbolism this way:

> His red garment signifies the devil's blood sacrifices; the royal crown signifies sin, which ruled the world [as a tyrant]; the white cloth in his hands with the twelve scrolls means the twelve Apostles, who brought light to the whole world with their teaching.[1]

The contrast is monumental: Before Christ, before the inauguration of His kingdom of light, the kingdoms of shadow reigned. But now, by the Spirit, the light and life of Christ are unleashed into the world, and the darkness cannot overcome it. The old, dark thrones have been overturned, razed by the shining power of the gospel.

REFLECT AND MEDITATE

Reflect upon the grandeur of the Holy Dove, the One who hovered over the chaotic tempest in the beginning, the One who descends from heaven and shines His light so that our whole person might be illuminated, that we may even catch on fire.

And meditate upon that time of darkness, both inner darkness and the darkness in the world, unilluminated by the giver of life.

Consider all the ways the Holy Spirit empowers us for life and kingdom work: to pray and guide, to support and make pilgrimage, to act in love and remain in Christ.

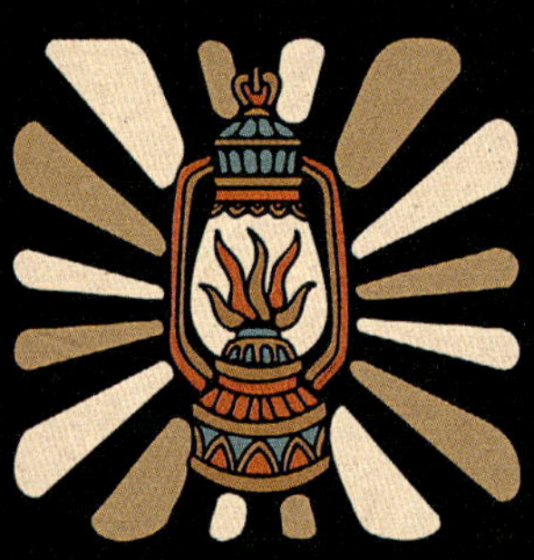

. . . WHO PROCEEDS FROM THE FATHER
[AND THE SON] . . .

DAY 29

This promised Holy Spirit, who is God, the giver of life, proceeds from the Father. Just as the Son is *begotten* from all eternity, so, too, the Spirit *proceeds* from the Father from all eternity. This is Trinitarian theology at its core: the Father is the Source, the Son is begotten, and the Spirit proceeds.[1]

This proceeding is a gift and an expression of unity. Here we begin to glimpse the full picture—at least, as much as the finite mind can—of the one unified work of the triune God.

Consider the acts of creation finding their source in the Father, accomplished through the Son and done by the Spirit. And consider the acts of redemption and new creation: The Father sends the Son, the Son accomplishes the mission, and the Spirit applies the life-giving work within us. Three persons, one nature, one will. Unity without fusion, distinction without separation.

This gift of the Spirit, this sending, is the fulfillment of Jesus' promise that He will remain with us, even to the end of the age. Jesus said it is better that He goes, for the Helper will come (John 16:7). This is the beginning of new creation. The old has gone, and the new has come (2 Corinthians 5:17).

The very breath of God, proceeding from the Father, now fills our mortal bodies and reconstitutes our lives. We are no longer wanderers in a dying world; we are living temples, and we are carried by the wind of His endless love.

REFLECT AND MEDITATE

Reflect upon the one will of the triune God, always united in love.

Meditate upon what Jesus meant in John 16:7 when He said it is better for Him to go away for a while and for Him to send the precious Holy Spirit.

Ponder what it means to be re-created, reconstituted by the giver of life, a gift that transforms.

WHO PROCEEDS FROM THE FATHER

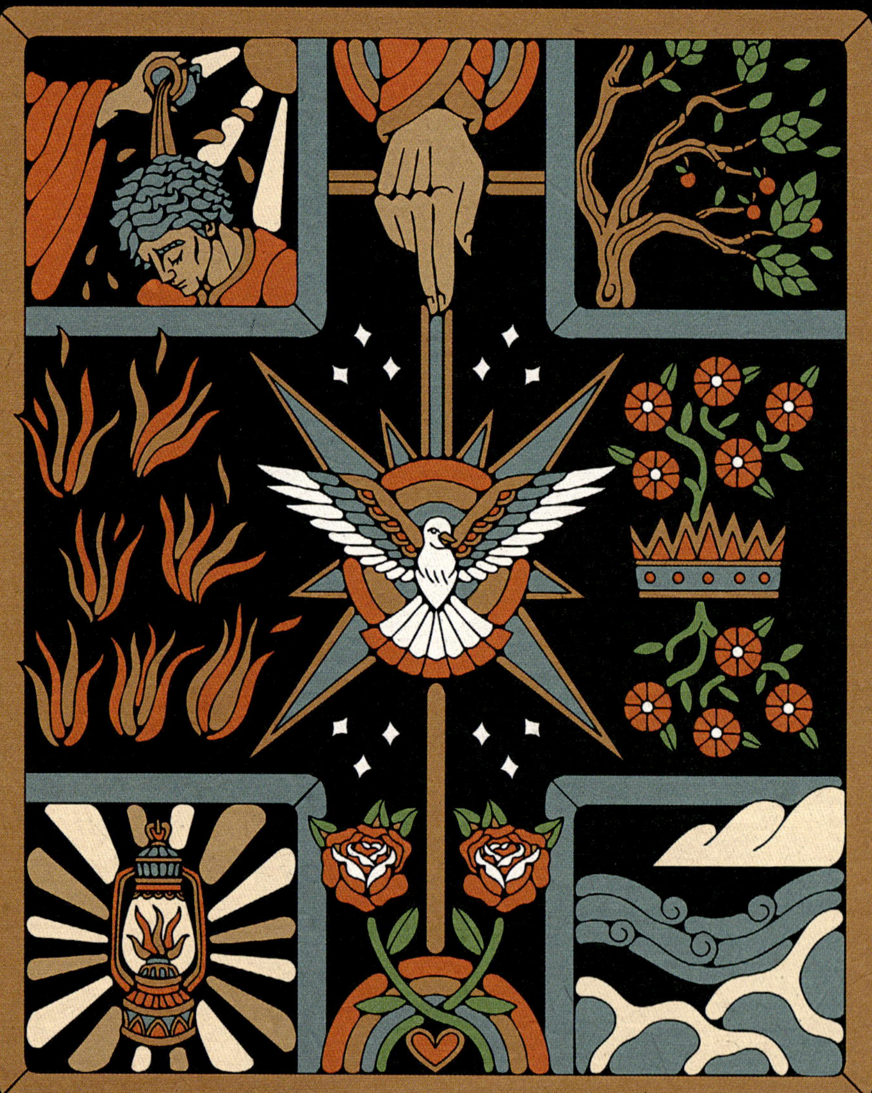

DAY 30

This image weaves together themes and motifs from all of Scripture, presenting them as a single and unified gift: the gift of the Father and the Son.

In the center, we see the Divine Hand—the Father Almighty—sending forth the Spirit. Eight rays emanate from the Holy Dove, symbolizing the people of God.

The top left image is a symbol of anointing, of being filled with the Spirit, and of having all knowledge (1 John 2:20).

Beneath this are the seven torches of Revelation 4:5, and these blazing lamps are an expression of the Holy Spirit.

The bottom left displays an image of a burning lantern, for the Spirit is the bringer of light. And adjacent is the Holy Spirit, hovering over the chaotic waters, the ancient image from Genesis 1, bringing order from a formless void.

Above this, on the right-hand side of the image, a crown of nine flowers blooms, each flower symbolizing one of the nine gifts of the Spirit (1 Corinthians 12:4–11), given to manifest God's presence in the world.

At the top right of the piece is a tree that sways in the breath of the Spirit, the unseen wind moving through the leaves. Here is the mystery Jesus spoke of: "The wind blows where it wishes, and you hear the sound of it, but cannot tell where it comes from and where it goes. So is everyone who is born of the Spirit" (John 3:8 NKJV).

REFLECT AND MEDITATE

Reflect upon the works of the Spirit, the One who fills us and empowers us for ministry. The One who bursts forth in flames before the throne of God. The One who brings light to our lives. The One who makes order out of chaos. The One who gives us gifts. The One who works within us in unseen ways, transforming us and making us like the Son.

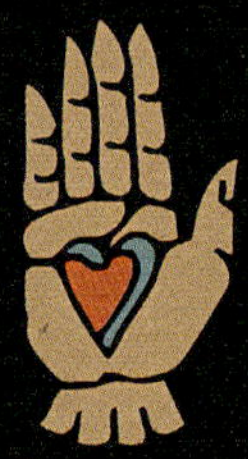

. . . WHO TOGETHER WITH THE FATHER AND THE SON
IS WORSHIPPED AND GLORIFIED . . .

DAY 31

The Creed makes certain that anyone reading or reciting it will not forget that the Holy Spirit, as God, is to be worshipped, adored, and glorified, just as we do with the Father and the Son. The Father, the Son, and the Spirit are inseparable and should be revered and honored together as our triune God.

We worship one God, baptized into His triunity, in the name of the Father, and the Son, and the Holy Spirit. We glorify the Trinity, and we celebrate a triune victory over sin and death. No being is lower or higher than the other; they are coequal, consubstantial.

And yet, oftentimes, the Holy Spirit goes unworshipped in our lives, for He always seeks to glorify the Son, to point to Him:

> However, when He, the Spirit of truth, has come, He will guide you into all truth; for He will not speak on His own authority, but whatever He hears He will speak; and He will tell you things to come. He will glorify Me, for He will take of what is Mine and declare it to you. (John 16:13–14 NKJV)

And yet it is this Spirit who watches over us while we rest, this same Spirit who comforts with His presence in every loss, who whispers to us internally through every storm and torrent of life, and fills us with the strength of God. He, too, is to be magnified and worshipped.

REFLECT AND MEDITATE

Take a moment to thank the Holy Spirit for all His unseen work in your life, all the moments you were carried when you thought you walked alone.

Reflect on the times the Spirit comforted you, taught you, or strengthened you without demanding to be seen, and give Him praise.

Worship the Spirit directly, not just for the gifts He gives but also for who He is: the Lord and giver of life.

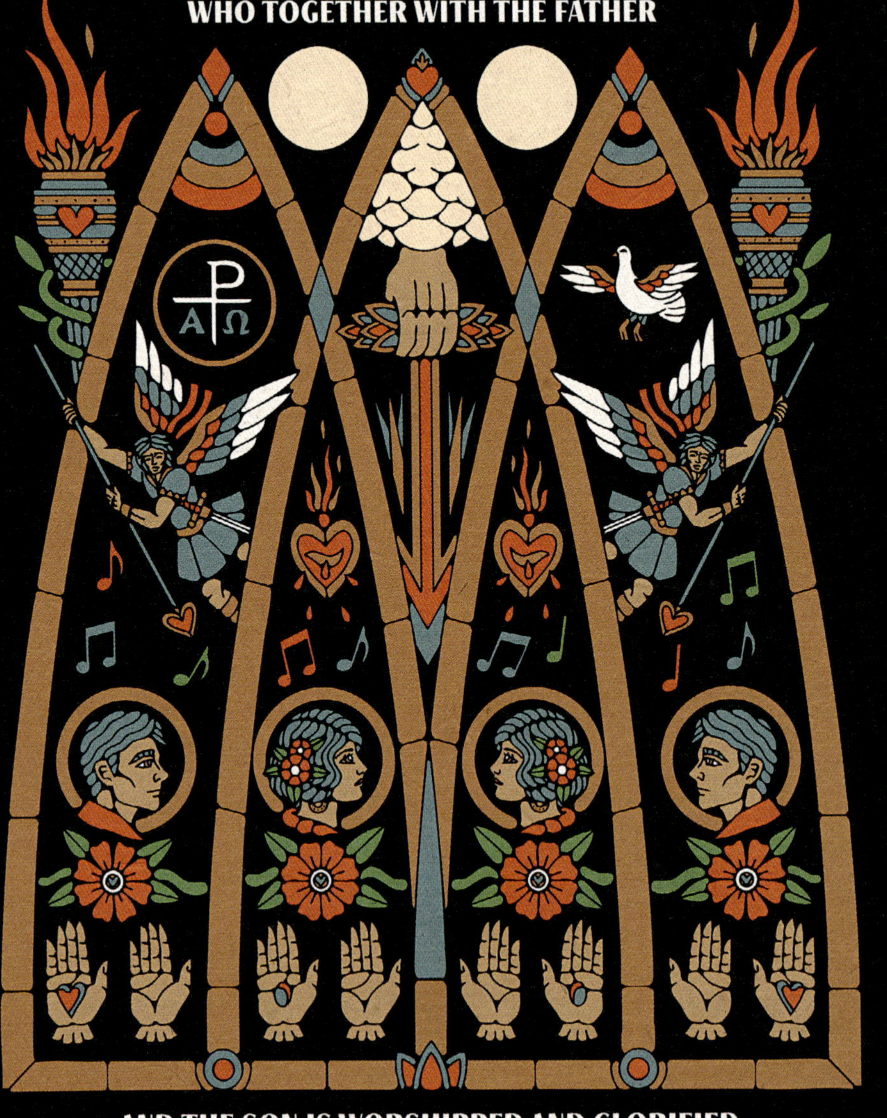
WHO TOGETHER WITH THE FATHER
AND THE SON IS WORSHIPPED AND GLORIFIED

DAY 32

This piece seeks to capture the *togetherness* of the Trinity as three overlapping stained glass arches within one church. Of course, no image or analogy can ever fully contain the mystery of the triune God. Every human symbol falls short, but even so, these glimpses can lead us closer to wonder and worship. Above the arches are the sun and moon, depicting the Trinity in the heavens, glorified above all. Framing either side are torches held fast by vines, symbolizing the Light of the World that gives life.

The left arch is a representation of Christ, begotten of the Father. The *Chi Rho* symbol, together with the alpha and omega, speak of the divinity of Christ. The right arch is a representation of the Holy Spirit, who proceeds from the Father. The dove here reminds us of our Lord's baptism and the descent at Pentecost. The rainbows in each arch symbolize the throne of God—suggesting that both the Son and the Spirit are fully and truly God. In the center arch is the Father Almighty, reaching down with a wreath of victory, sending His blessed light to the earth.

On either side are angels with spears of love. These are messengers who proclaim the glory of the triune God, and the saints below them, depicted with halos, are joining in the song of worship. Beneath these saints are flowers, which here represent works of love done in union with the Godhead. And at the bottom are hands lifted in praise and worship of the triune God.

REFLECT AND MEDITATE

Reflect upon the unity of the Trinity, and consider why God is worthy of praise and adoration.

Consider His mighty works; join with all of creation in a song of worship.

Consider how the unity and love within the Trinity are meant to shape how we live and why we are to be self-giving and honoring, delighting in others.

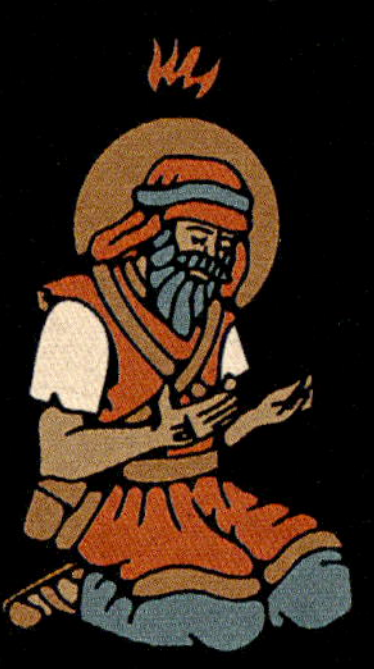

. . . WHO SPOKE THROUGH THE PROPHETS . . .

DAY 33

It is this Holy Spirit, God Himself, who has spoken *through* the prophets.

God has spoken to humanity, and He has done so by His Spirit *through* a prophetic voice. He has whispered to us the hidden joys of heaven, the coming of the King, the great narrative of faith. This is the story of God: a single, ongoing message to His people. A tapestry of redemption, of hope, of salvation, and of life everlasting.

We read from the mouths of the prophets Isaiah, Jeremiah, and Ezekiel, "The Lord says . . ." and we can be sure that God is truly speaking through them. Their utterance is His utterance.

We believe that the Holy Spirit has inspired many, from kings and shepherds to fishermen and tax collectors, weaving the threads of the tapestry of the story of God together. "No prophecy ever came by the will of man, but men spoke from God as they were being carried along by the Holy Spirit" (2 Peter 1:21 EHV).

God is not distant; He is telling His story through real lives and real voices. He is the source of His own revelation, and He Himself, in the Person of the Spirit, continues to speak to His Church. God's revelation is preserved for us, in part, within our holy Scriptures: the written words of prophets, apostles, and witnesses.

Scripture says it is "God-breathed" (2 Timothy 3:16 NIV), which means God is its principal author, and it is inspired by the Holy Spirit. The same Spirit who hovered over the waters of creation, who is the life that animated Adam, and who set the prophets' hearts on fire. And as we read the Scriptures, we can hear the Spirit telling us the great story of God.

In Ephesians 5:19, Paul spoke of being filled with the Spirit and of learning to speak to one another with psalms and hymns and songs of the Spirit. In a sister passage, Paul described the same fruit, songs and hymns, but this time he said it comes by letting "the Word of Christ dwell in you richly" (Colossians 3:16 NKJV).

The connection is purposeful. The Word and the Spirit are united. The Spirit does not bring a different message than Christ; He reminds us, teaches us, and draws us deeper into the one great story. Just as the Spirit spoke through the prophets of old to proclaim the coming Messiah, so now He speaks to us through the written Word. He announces that the Messiah has come and will come again.

It is this great story that the Spirit has spoken to us and continues to speak to us, that at last, our Redeemer lives and will stand upon the earth, and His kingdom will have no end.

REFLECT AND MEDITATE

Reflect upon how God spoke at first through prophets, then through His Son, and even in His written Word to us. Consider what it would have meant to hear a prophet speak and to have heard Jesus speak. Then consider that God's Spirit resides within you, speaking.

Ponder the great and unified message of God through the ages. No mistakes, no lies. Just the revelation of God to us, that He is everything we need for life and godliness.

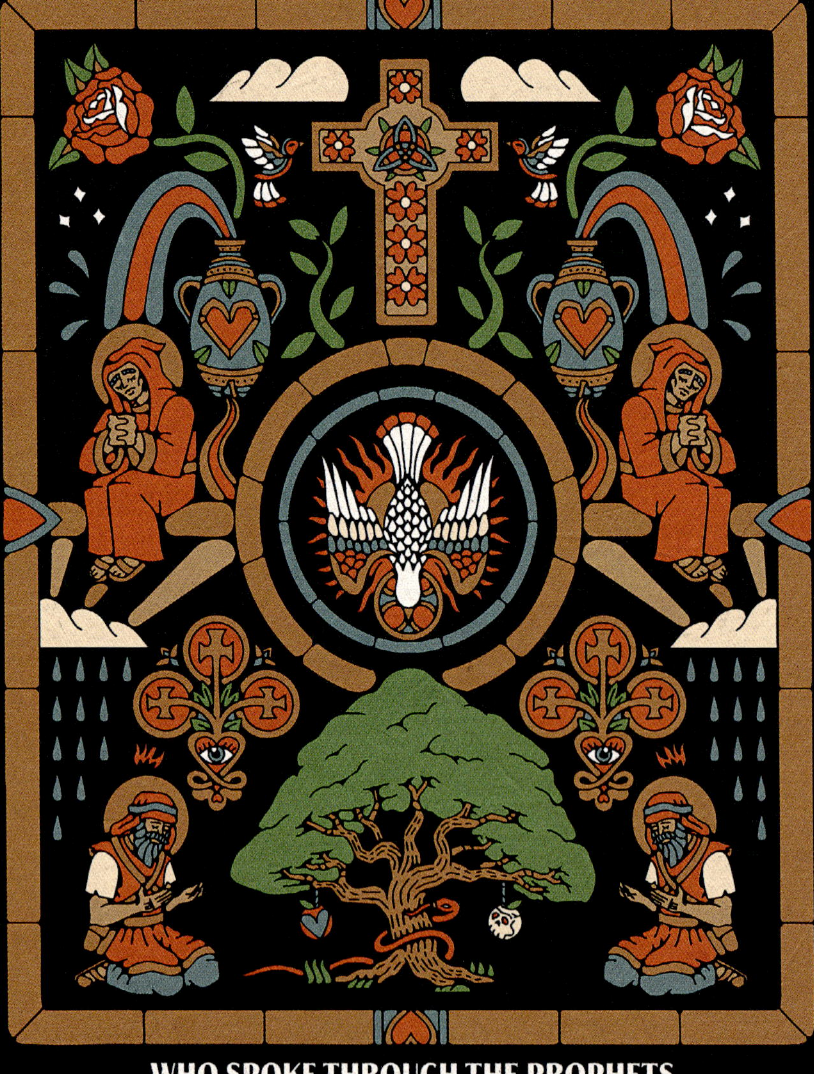

WHO SPOKE THROUGH THE PROPHETS

DAY 34

This piece centers around a shining depiction of the Holy Spirit as a dove. Framing the piece are two prophets, kneeling, with tongues of fire above their heads. It is through this prayer, this union, that these prophets are filled with God's Spirit so as to speak His words.

Between them is the Tree, in Eden, whose fruit holds the knowledge of good and evil, and a Serpent coils around its base. It is here, at the roots of this tree, that humanity falls headlong into the grave, and it is here that the words of God toward humanity turn to redemption.

The prophets cry out with promises: that a Savior will come, that death will be undone, that the wounds of Eden will be healed. Their voices are a testimony to both our deep need and God's deeper mercy. We need a Savior to rescue us from the domain of death and darkness. Framing the tree is a symbol of the Trinity erupting in love and set out for salvation.

Above are urns filled with anointing oil, flowing up and washing over two praying prophets, seated above the clouds. Those same urns are bursting through the "old wineskins" (Matthew 9:17 NKJV) and flowing like a river, filling the clouds, which water down below.

This carries the idea that all of creation speaks of God, day and night proclaiming Him, because they were created by God.

Up from these urns grow two flowers, and lighting upon them are two swallows. These flowers represent life and growth, and the swallows call to mind that God provides, even for these. So how much more will He provide for us?

At the top is a depiction of a cross laden in roses. This revelation, this speaking through the prophets, points to the great story of Jesus, the Christ, who came for our sake and for our salvation.

REFLECT AND MEDITATE

Meditate on all the ways God has spoken His prophetic message to us of a Promised Savior. Meditate on all the other ways He speaks: through His Word, through creation, through gentle promptings, and through His Church.

Reflect upon the language of creation, singing because it bears the divine imprint. Think about learning to hear its language.

Consider how everything speaks of Christ—all stories culminate in Him—and consider how the Holy Spirit is always guiding us to Christ.

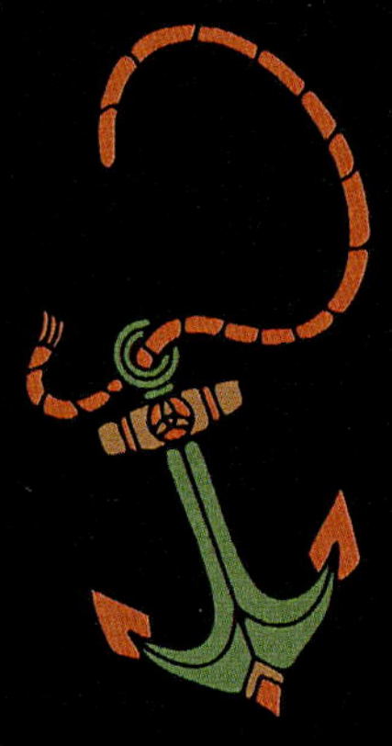

WE BELIEVE IN ONE,
HOLY, CATHOLIC, AND
APOSTOLIC CHURCH.

DAY 35

The Creed now turns from the triune God to the Church.

This Church was set up by Christ. "Upon this rock," He said to Peter, "I will build my church; and the gates of hell shall not prevail against it" (Matthew 16:18 KJV). And He built the Church upon His own life, death, and resurrection. This is the Church of the living God, the pillar and foundation of truth. This is the new covenant community, the covenant made by the life-giving blood of Jesus, the community formed by the power of His Spirit.

And if Jesus is the builder, then we are the living stones. We are gathered into one body, of one faith, to bear His light and life out into the world.

In the New Testament conception, God does His work among His gathered community. This is where God is made manifest: in the Lord's Supper, in the preaching of the Word, in psalms and hymns and songs, in the gifts of the Spirit. In 1 Corinthians 12:12, Paul spoke of this Church as a unified body. And just as a body is unsevered and joined together, so, too, is the Church under Christ, who is our head.

We believe in one Church. That is, Jesus has made one *institution*. One body. His bride.

We believe that the Church is *holy*. We believe that the Church is devoted to the mission and worship of Jesus and that we who make up the Church are committed to the spreading of His kingdom. Holiness goes beyond ideas of ethics and morality, though it includes those. Holiness is primarily about loyalty. And this Church, if it is to be called a Church at all, remains loyal to God in all things.

We believe in the *catholic* Church. *Catholic* here means "universal," that is, the body of Christ, now and through all ages. The Church exists all over the world, and each true church is a part of the body of Christ, unified under Him.

We believe in the *apostolic* Church. We seek to maintain the truth handed down to us by the apostles. The Church is built upon their foundation, with Jesus as the chief cornerstone (Ephesians 2:20). It is the apostles' words, written down and from their mouths, that we follow, and our heritage is rich. We can look back in time, through so many books, and read about the apostles and their disciples and what they taught about Jesus, the Christ, and the good news of His kingdom.

This is the Church we believe in, the bride of Christ. And now, it is the time of *betrothal*, the time before the great wedding, before the marriage supper of the Lamb. And during this time, the bride is to remain faithful, to prepare herself, and we do so by the power of the Spirit.

REFLECT AND MEDITATE

Reflect upon the one Church, unified as one body is unified. Think of all that divides us, and consider the heart of Christ for His Church.

Reflect upon the Church as holy and loyal, and consider how that loyalty expresses itself: in doctrine, in obedience, in ethics and morality, in seeking to be a representation of Christ, His body remaining on earth, through us.

Reflect upon the Church as catholic, existing in all places and in all times, universal and yet still together.

Reflect upon the Church as apostolic, established on that which was passed down by Jesus and His followers and our great Christian heritage.

WE BELIEVE IN ONE, HOLY,

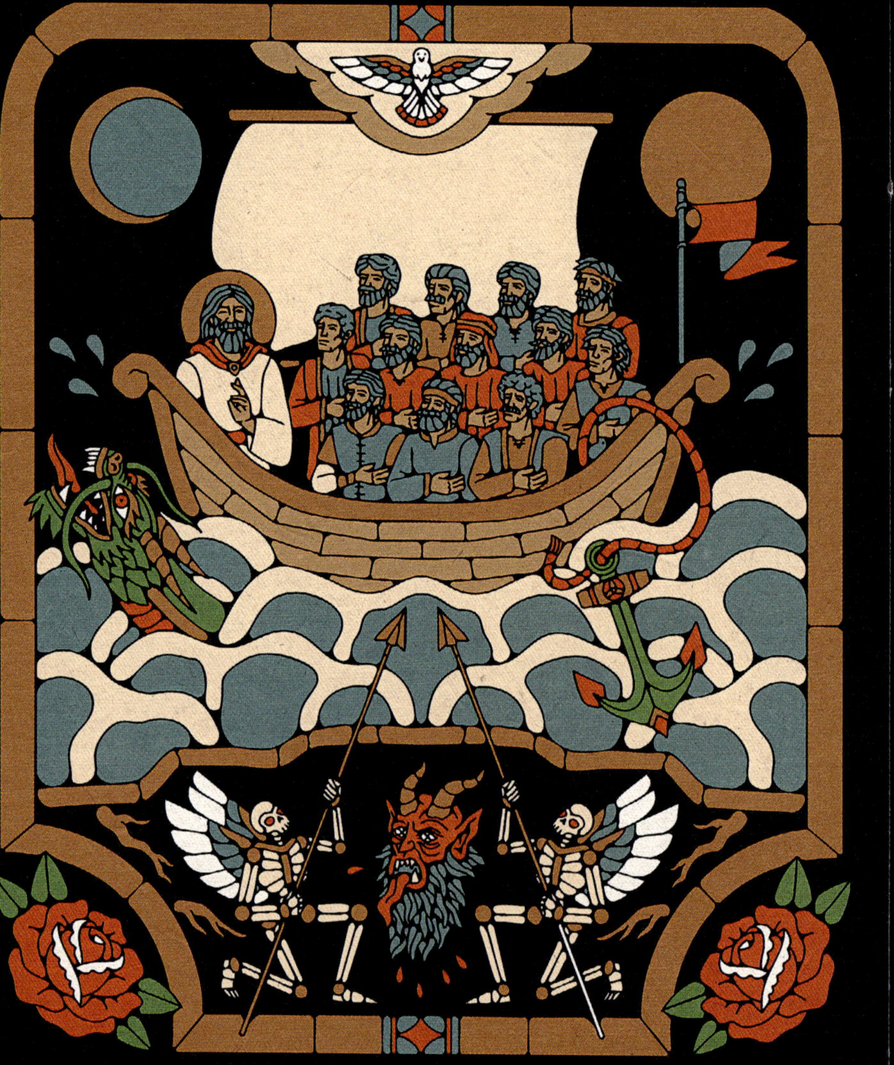

CATHOLIC, AND APOSTOLIC CHURCH.

DAY 36

This piece centers around the Church as a ship, as an ark, building on an idea found from the early Church father Jerome. This Church, this new covenant community, this *one body*, carries all those who are in Christ over the floodwaters. Inside this ship, at the helm, is Jesus, who guides us safely through every storm to the shores of eternity. With Him are the twelve apostles, who represent the Church. This conception has been depicted in Church art many times.

Above the ship, filling the sails, is the Holy Spirit, who hovered over the chaotic waters in the beginning, who hovered over Jesus at His baptism, and who now breathes life into the Church, keeping her moving, united with Christ, and leading her home.

In the chaotic waters is the Leviathan, an ancient image of chaos and resistance to the order of God, and it is over this chaos that the Church sails. There is also an anchor, a symbol of hope, sure and steadfast—the hope set before us, hope in God and in the life to come.

From under the earth we see the gates of hell that seek to prevail against the Church, winged skeletons with spears raised up in defiance, and the severed head of Satan, the Church's great enemy, between them. These gates will not prevail, no matter what attack comes, and no weapons that are formed against the Church will prosper (Isaiah 54:17).

REFLECT AND MEDITATE

Reflect upon what it means to be in the Church instituted by Christ. Consider the unity through the ages, consider that Christ is the captain of our faith, and consider that He is leading us to the true promised land.

Consider all the ways the Enemy seeks to destroy the Church, to sink her, sever her, and uproot her. There are times when we, knowingly or not, seek the destruction of the Church as well, by word or action. Pray and seek to be for the Church, the bride of Christ.

Reflect upon why the gates of hell will not prevail. And consider that it is Jesus who keeps us safe from all manner of hell, from every tempest, and that He guides us home.

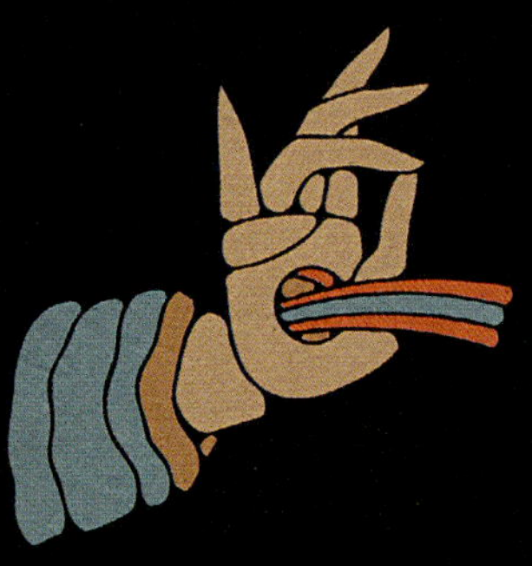

WE CONFESS ONE BAPTISM FOR THE FORGIVENESS OF SINS.

DAY 37

The Creed moves to another *confession*, which we make in unison: *one* baptism for the forgiveness of sins.

Baptism is about regeneration—the new life that comes from God by the Spirit. Baptism is our exodus and our crossing over.

God's people fled the captivity and tyranny of Egypt through the Red Sea, up and out into a free and new life. So, too, does the Church, God's true people, find salvation and new life through the waters, up and out of the captivity of death and into the freedom of Christ.

And just as Israel crossed the Jordan into the promised land, so, too, does the Church, the true Israel of God, pass through the waters, looking forward to the true promised land.

The Creed quotes from Ephesians 4:5: "one Lord, one faith, one baptism" (NKJV). This one baptism is for all people. There is no different baptism for Jews or Gentiles, for slave or free, for male or female. Through water and Spirit, we are all unified with Christ; through water and Spirit, we are joined to His death and raised into His life.

We are baptized in the name of the triune God—Father, Son,

and Spirit. It is a sacramental act, a means of grace, a participation in the life and death of Christ.

In Acts 2:38, Peter said:

> Repent and be baptized, every one of you, in the name of Jesus Christ for the forgiveness of your sins. And you will receive the gift of the Holy Spirit. (NIV)

Baptism is about being united to Christ, clothed in Him, as Paul wrote in Galatians 3:27:

> For all of you who were baptized into Christ have clothed yourselves with Christ. (NIV)

Baptism is the sacramental beginning of our new identity. It is about obedience. It is about death and rebirth, as Paul proclaimed in Titus 3:

> But when the kindness and the love of God our Savior toward man appeared, not by works of righteousness which we have done, but according to His mercy He saved us, through the washing of regeneration and renewing of the Holy Spirit. (vv. 4–5 NKJV)

In baptism, our sins are washed away. We are made new. We step into the life of the Son.

REFLECT AND MEDITATE

Reflect upon baptism as the sign of the new covenant, that the whole Church in all of history has confessed this one baptism, given by our Lord.

Reflect upon the symbolism of the waters, leaving the slavery of sin and death and emerging up and out and into the promised land.

Consider the kindness of God, washing away our sins and renewing us by His Holy Spirit.

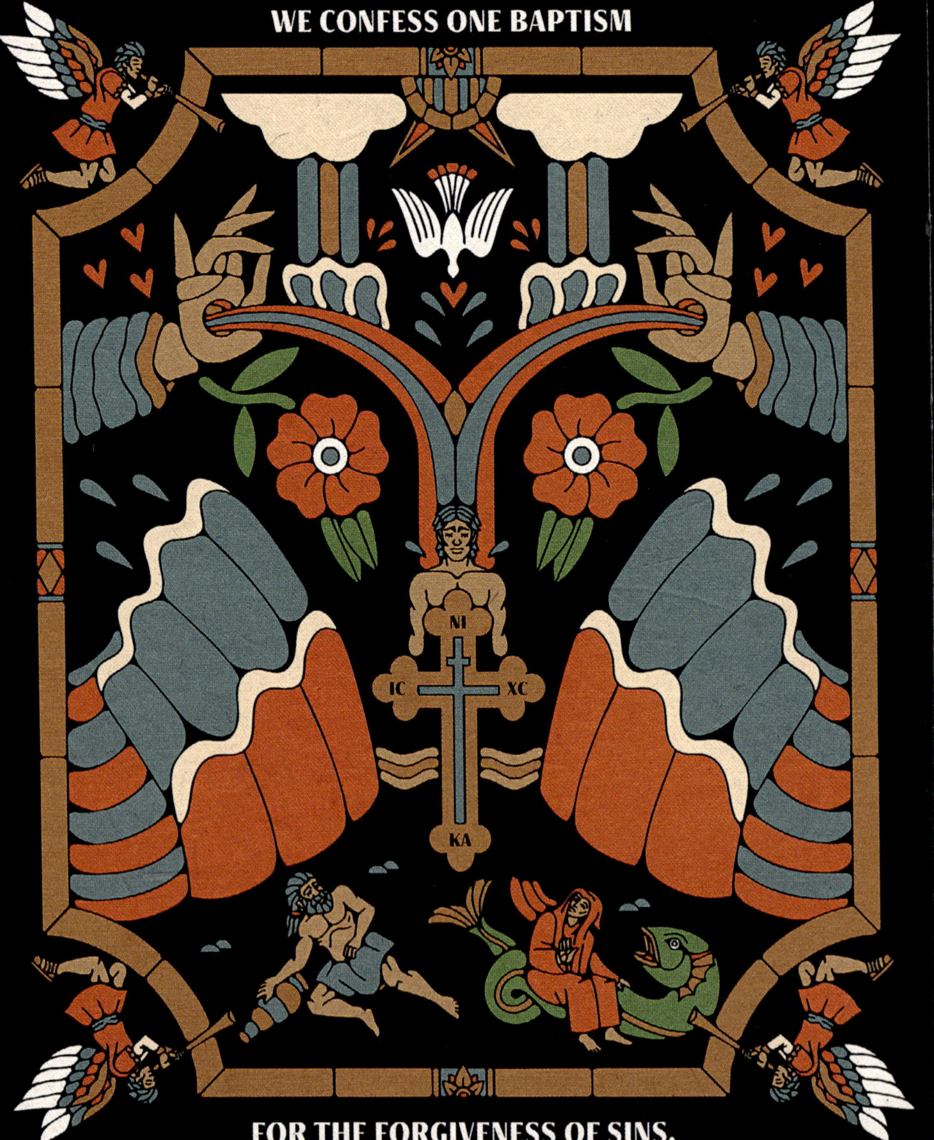
WE CONFESS ONE BAPTISM
NI
IC
XC
KA
FOR THE FORGIVENESS OF SINS.

DAY 38

At the center of this piece is a person being baptized into Christ, symbolized by the cross and the inscription *IC XC NIKA*, or "Jesus Christ Conquers." Beside this person are the waters, split at the Red Sea, mixed water and blood—a depiction of our own escape from captivity and captivity itself being slain.

At the bottom of the piece are two symbols, the Sea and the Jordan. These are depicted in many Eastern Orthodox icons of Jesus' baptism, which portray Psalm 114:3: "The sea saw it and fled; Jordan turned back" (NKJV).

In these icons, the Jordan and the sea flee from Jesus—not because He needed to be purified but because He purifies them. Christ steps into the waters not to be cleansed but to cleanse, to sanctify all of creation, to make the waters of baptism a font of divine grace.

Above the parted sea are Christ's hands, pouring down water and blood, another symbol that we are baptized into Christ. We are buried with Him in baptism and raised with Him (Romans 6:4).

At the top of the piece is the glory of the Father, a dove representing the Holy Spirit, and clouds raining down blessings. Baptism is done in the name of the Father, the Son, and the Holy Spirit. We are baptized into the family of God and are united unto Him, and with baptism come all the blessings of that union.

REFLECT AND MEDITATE

Reflect upon your own baptism and how you descended into the waters and emerged into newness of life.

Consider how Christ entered the waters not for Himself but for you—to purify, to bless, to claim your life as His own.

Reflect on your baptism as the mark of Christ's victory over sin and death, the seal of your place within the new covenant community.

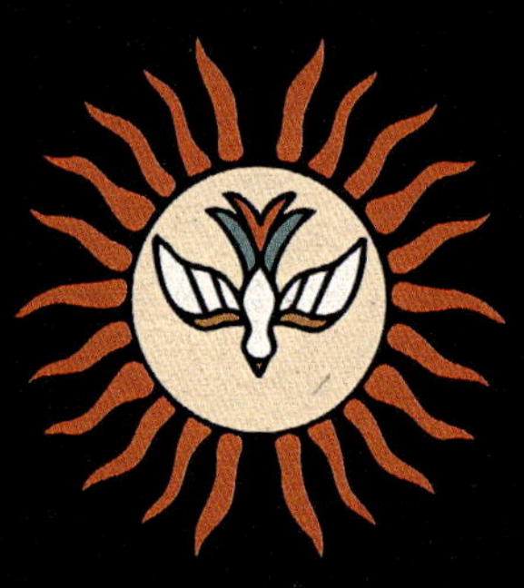

WE LOOK FOR THE RESURRECTION OF THE DEAD,
AND THE LIFE OF THE AGE TO COME.
AMEN.

DAY 39

Our last confession and declaration is our great hope: the resurrection of the dead, the life to come in the new heaven and new earth. Jesus said:

> I am the resurrection and the life. The one who believes in me will live, even though they die; and whoever lives by believing in me will never die. Do you believe this? (John 11:25–26 NIV)

In His own death and resurrection, Jesus has become the firstfruits for all who have fallen asleep. He is the proof that death is dead, proof that the old wooden doors that hung heavy over the grave have been shattered. Proof that we, too, can emerge from death with Him.

For those who are in Christ—united with Him in faith—we will be raised with Him. In the twinkling of an eye, that which is corruptible will be made incorruptible, the mortal will put on immortality, and death will be swallowed by victory. Forever and in fullness.

This fullness of life is the New Eden, the garden city, the place of all longings fulfilled.

In *Mere Christianity*, C. S. Lewis wrote, "If I find in myself a desire which no experience in this world can satisfy, the most probable explanation is that I was made for another world."[1] And indeed we are. We have been made for a new world. And one day, by grace, we will call it home.

This is the consummation of the kingdom, a fulfillment of our prayers: "Thy kingdom come, Thy will be done in earth, as it is in heaven" (Matthew 6:10 KJV).

In this coming kingdom there will be no need of sun, for Christ Himself—Light of light—will be our illumination. There will be no sea, for chaos will be no more. These are theological claims, not astronomical or geological. There will still be sunsets and beams cutting through branches; we will still feel the salt spray of the sea. The meaning behind these theological statements is clear: Our true light, by which we live and see, will be Christ. And the deep chaos, the tumultuous sea and its monsters, will be conquered and calmed.

And this is what gives us courage, not that the storms will stop but that they cannot last forever. Every rough sea we face, every shadow that looms over us, every ache—all of it is temporary.

The Light has come, and the darkness cannot overcome it. The old order of things has passed away, and now it is the time of fullness and participation; the time of promises realized, of true unity and communion with God.

REFLECT AND MEDITATE

Consider Christ, who is the pioneer of your faith. Imagine Him making the way for you and leading you up out of the grave, through this sojourn of life, and then into the World to come.

Imagine the place of all longings fulfilled, imagine all your deepest desires, and imagine how God will satisfy them.

Reflect upon the new order of things and all the things that mark our lives now that will pass away. Reflect upon what it means to be faithful now, in the midst of this old order, and consider the joy of rest in the new order.

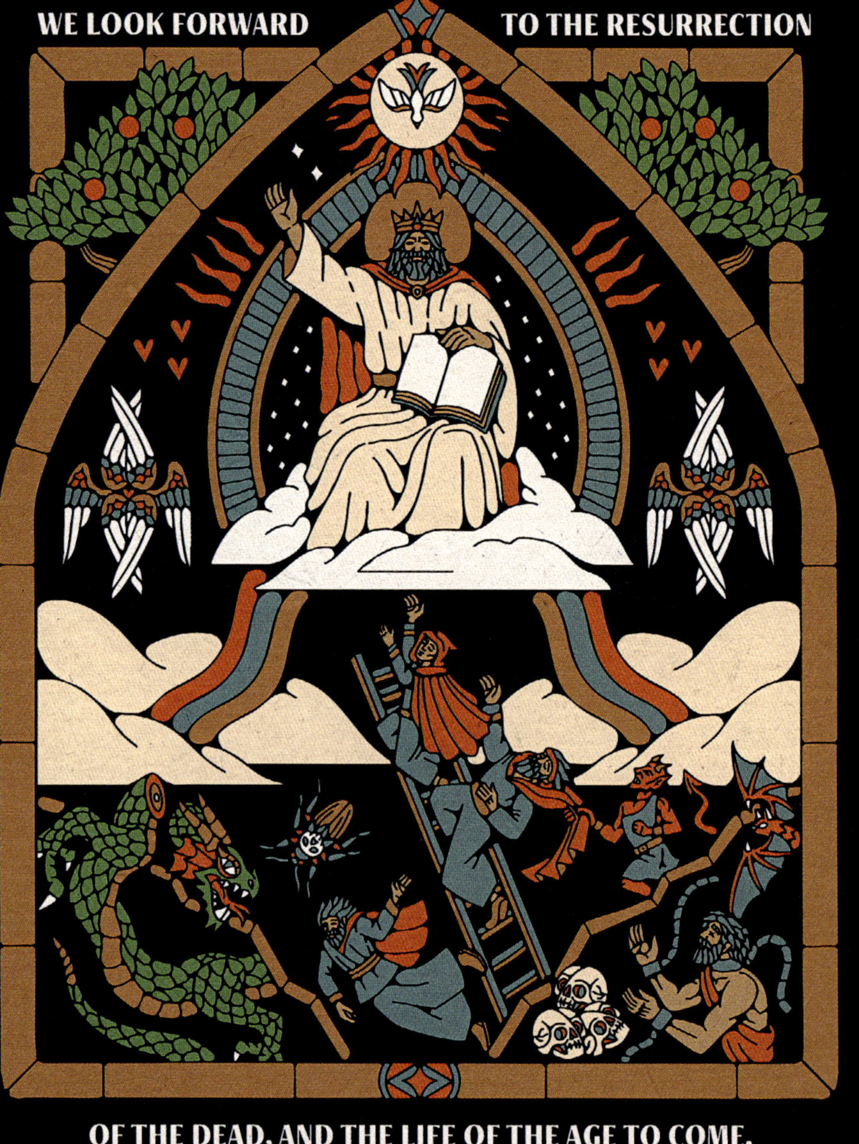
WE LOOK FORWARD TO THE RESURRECTION
OF THE DEAD, AND THE LIFE OF THE AGE TO COME.

DAY 40

At the top of this piece is the victorious King, Jesus, the Alpha and Omega, seated on His throne in the heavens. From this throne flow rivers, wild and blue and bright. These waters feed trees that blossom with all good fruit, fulfilling the vision of Revelation 22:2.

Beside Jesus are the seraphim and the heavenly host, singing praise to His glorious name. Framing the piece are mature trees whose leaves are for the healing of the nations.

The clouds are shining, fed by the river of God, representing the life of the new Kingdom and the full union of heaven and earth.

Climbing up into the heavens are the saints—those who have followed Jesus, put their trust in Him, and been loyal to His life. They seek to seize hold of His sacrificial love by faith, day after day.

There is an already and not-yet dimension to this piece.

Even now we are called to climb. Our life here is not passive; it is a striving onward and upward, rejecting the powers of sin and death and hell. It is a daily choice to ascend Jacob's Ladder, to seek the face of the Most High.

And not everyone makes it.

There are those who leave the path, those who reject the path.

Those who refuse the life of God will repeat the great consequence of Eden: exile from the Tree of Life. And in that exile, they will meet death. This is depicted in the bottom of the image, humans void of the life of God, emaciated, starving, imprisoned in the domain of death. To reject life is to embrace annihilation.

And in the lower left is that Great Dragon, Satan, defeated and cast into all hellfire. His head is severed, his wings broken, for the old order has passed away.

A contrast exists in most Christian art depicting this great consummation, a hierarchy of experience. Those in Christ, who have tasted the heavenly gift, will live with Him forever. Those who reject Him, reject His life, are cast out. Outside of life, there is only death and darkness, and even those will one day be consumed.

We understand reality by contrasts, and here is the greatest of all contrasts: Blessed are those who run toward the light. Woe to those who flee from it.

The King has conquered. The curse is broken. The dead shall rise. And the long ache of our hearts will finally be satisfied in the radiance of His face. We are waiting for the coming dawn. We look forward to the resurrection of the dead and the life of the world to come.

And in the Nicene Creed, in our history, there is one final encouragement:

Bless the Son. Confess Him as Lord. And live.

REFLECT AND MEDITATE

Reflect upon the life to come, and let it influence and impact your daily living. Consider all the ways in which true union with Jesus transforms your current days.

Take a moment to bless the Son and confess Him as Lord. Take a moment to reflect on the full narrative of the Creed.

Sit in silence before the might and glory of God.

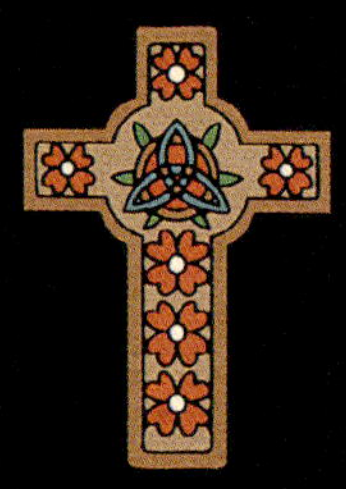

WAYS OF BEING

When I first sat down to write this book, I wrote one short phrase, and it kept circling in my mind for weeks: *We did not form the Creed. The Creed formed us.*

Yes, the Church compiled the Creed—listing and clarifying what has always been the faith. But the Church didn't invent these doctrines. We did not create them or form them. They exist in God whether we name them or not.

This Creed has shaped us. It has been the solid ground beneath our feet for centuries, a guiding lamp to lead the wandering and the faithful. It is the foundation of our faith.

It is through these confessions that we are remade, day by day, into the image of the triune God. The Creed forms us—heart, soul, mind, and strength.

Our journey through the Creed has not been primarily intellectual; it has been sacramental, a way of being shaped by beauty and presence. Truth set on fire by beauty.

I hope you learned something along the way.

More than that, I hope truth found good soil in your heart. I hope these forty days became something *real*. A beckoning closer to the living God. A call to a new life. Preparation for all that comes next: a true harvest.

This Creed is ancient air. When you breathe it in, you breathe the wild and free life of God. It is the clean sea breeze of the ages rushing through the hills and valleys of history and filling our lungs. It is the scent of the coming kingdom. Through this Creed, you can, for a moment, live in that overlap—where heaven meets earth.

By the Creed you can ascend the mountain, and you can accept the invitation to know Him as we know one another—by presence, familiarity, communion, and loyalty.

My prayer is that somewhere along these pages, somewhere in the words and art, in the quiet times of prayer, God met you. That He revealed Himself to you. That He offered you His hand to hold, to guide you deeper into His life and deeper into loyalty. That He invited you to help carry His kingdom into the world.

I hope the Creed has formed you—or re-formed you—from the inside out. And I hope you descend this ancient mountain shining with the light of the Son, for you are His reflection in the world.

You are His.

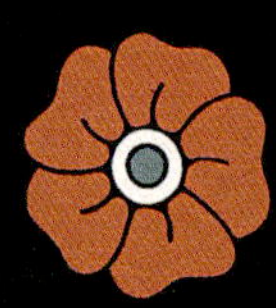

NOTES

LET THERE BE . . .

1. St. Augustine of Hippo, "Late Have I Loved You, Beauty So Ancient and So New!" Crossroads Initiative, August 27, 2023, crossroadsinitiative.com/media/articles/late-have-i-loved-you-beauty-augustine_feast_august-28/.
2. St. Gregory of Nyssa, quoted in Theophan Whitfield, "(16) A Shovel Full of . . ." Saint Nicholas Orthodox Church, accessed June 3, 2025, orthodoxsalem.com/abba-anthony-16-20.

WAYS OF SEEING

1. C. S. Lewis, introduction to *On the Incarnation*, by St. Athanasius (St. Vladimir's Seminary Press, 1993), 5.
2. C. S. Lewis, *Till We Have Faces: A Myth Retold* (HarperOne, 2017), 86.

BY WORD AND IMAGE

1. Vladimir Lossky, *The Mystical Theology of the Eastern Church* (St. Vladimir's Seminary Press, 2002), 9.
2. Gerard Manley Hopkins, "God's Grandeur," *Poetry Foundation*, accessed June 3, 2025, poetryfoundation.org/poems/44395/gods-grandeur.
3. "Letter of His Holiness Pope John Paul II to Artists," The Holy See, 1999, vatican.va/content/john-paul-ii/en/letters/1999/documents/hf_jp-ii_let_23041999_artists.html.

INTO THE WILDERNESS

1. John A. McGuckin, *Prayer Book of the Early Christians* (Paraclete Press, 2017), 157–58.

DAY 1

1. St. Athanasius, *On the Incarnation of the Word* (St. Vladimir's Seminary Press, 1993), 28.

DAY 2

1. G. K. Chesterton, *The Everlasting Man* (Project Gutenberg, 2024), 107.
2. J. R. R. Tolkien, *The Silmarillion* (Morrow, 2022), and C. S. Lewis, *The Magician's Nephew* (HarperCollins, 2025).

DAY 3

1. G. K. Chesterton, *Orthodoxy* (Image Books, 1959), 60.

DAY 9

1. Hans Boersma, "God as Embodied: Christology and Participation in Saint Maximus the Confessor," *St. Vladimir's Theological Quarterly* 67, no. 1–2 (2023): 147–69.

DAY 13

1. Athanasius, quoted in Matthew A. Tsakanikas, "Saint Athanasius on Divinization," *Adoremus*, accessed June 3, 2025, adoremus.org/2024/05/saint-athanasius-on-divinization/.
2. C. S. Lewis, *Mere Christianity* (HarperOne, 2001), 199.

DAY 15

1. Athanasius, "Letter 61," ed. Kevin Knight, New Advent, accessed June 3, 2025, newadvent.org/fathers/2806061.htm.

DAY 19

1. C. S. Lewis, *God in the Dock: Essays on Theology and Ethics*, ed. Walter Hooper (Eerdmans, 1970), 67.

DAY 28

1. C_Schlesser, "Pentecost—Descent of the Holy Spirit," Classical Iconography Institute, May 19, 2024, classicaliconography.org/pentecost-descent-of-the-holy-spirit/.

DAY 29

1. This is the only real bit of controversy in the Creed—it was a major part of the schism that happened in 1054, between East and West

(the Orthodox and Roman Catholics). The controversy pertains to the phrase "and the Son," or *filioque*, and if it should be in the Creed at all. I have opted for the version of the Creed accepted by the ecumenical councils—less as a theological point and more for consistency concerning the nature of this book.

DAY 39

1. C. S. Lewis, *Mere Christianity* (HarperOne, 2001), 136–37.

ABOUT THE AUTHOR

Josh Nadeau is an artist and author from the West Coast of Canada. Beauty is his apologetic, and his work seeks to translate ancient ideas of embodying the transcendent for a modern time. His art and writing are invitations to reimagine the holy ordinary of everyday life under the beauty of Jesus.

He has appeared on numerous podcasts, written articles for magazines and websites, and created art for Jordan Peterson's *History of Western Civilization*, as well as for churches, musicians, and other organizations like The Chosen, Searock, Vuvivo, and the Daily Wire.

Josh has his undergrad in physics, a master's in theological studies, and a doctorate from the School of Hard Knocks. He is a husband to Aislinn and a father to Ransom. He spends his days reading, writing, bouldering, and trying to enjoy every good and perfect gift. Josh is the founder of Sword and Pencil and Every Day Saints.

Josh Nadeau

CREATOR OF SWORD AND PENCIL

Room for Good Things to Run Wild

HOW ORDINARY PEOPLE BECOME EVERY DAY SAINTS

Let Beauty Bring You Home

Embrace a Holy, Ordinary, Life of Wonder

You've bought the slogans, said the half-hearted prayers; you've gone through the motions and played the part on those humdrum Sundays. You've been stuck in that hamster-cage existence—a faith reduced to routine, a life reduced to survival. And you're looking for the promises of your faith to pull through.

Room for Good Things to Run Wild is the antidote to widespread Christian Malaise. If you feel like life is happening to you, that your faith has been reduced to trite platitudes, and that no matter how many new things you try, you still end up with a dissatisfying Christian life, this book offers relief from the mediocrity of Christian living through the sacred and satisfying journey of becoming an every day saint.

With literature, doctrine, art, raw life, illustrations, and living liturgy, Josh leads you across continents—Canada, England, Ireland, Spain—drawing you into what he calls the Holy Ordinary, the embracing of wild beauty of God, waking the soul and satisfying the body.

Heaven Meets Earth

Published by Thomas Nelson, 501 Nelson Place, Nashville, TN 37214, USA. Thomas Nelson is a registered trademark of HarperCollins Christian Publishing, Inc.

Published in association with Yates & Yates, www.yates2.com.

Cover art and interior art: Josh Nadeau

Thomas Nelson titles may be purchased in bulk for educational, business, fund-raising, or sales promotional use. For information, please email SpecialMarkets@ThomasNelson.com.

HarperCollins Publishers, Macken House, 39/40 Mayor Street Upper, Dublin 1, D01 C9W8, Ireland (https://www.harpercollins.com)

Cover design: Josh Nadeau
Interior design: Kristen Sasamoto

ISBN 978-1-4002-5437-8 (HC)
ISBN 978-1-4002-5438-5 (eBook)

Printed in India

25 26 27 28 29 30 RPI 10 9 8 7 6 5 4 3 2 1